STRIDES

Study Guide Book 1

Sandra McCandless Simons

Harcourt Brace Jovanovich, Inc.
Holt, Rinehart and Winston, Inc.
Orlando · Austin · San Diego · Chicago · Dallas · Toronto

Contents

Unit 1

Before you read	The Race to Dog Tail Island	1–7
After you read	The Race to Dog Tail Island	8–11
Before you read	The Pride of Madison High	12–18
After you read	The Pride of Madison High	19–20
Before you read	The Four-Fifteen Express	21–25
After you read	The Four-Fifteen Express	26–27
Before you read	Radio Sound Effects	28–31
After you read	Radio Sound Effects	32–35

Unit 2

Before you read	Sarah Tops	36–40
After you read	Sarah Tops	41–44
After you read	A Nation on Wheels	45–48
Before you read	An American Hero	49–54
After you read	An American Hero	55–57
Before you read	A Change for the Better	58–63
After you read	A Change for the Better	64–67

Unit 3

Before you read	Volcano!	68–72
After you read	Volcano!	73–77
After you read	What Will They Think of Next?	78–81
Before you read	Twenty-Two	82–89
After you read	Twenty-Two	90–93
Before you read	The Trap	94–98
After you read	The Trap	99–102

Unit 4

Before you read	Daring Mission	103–107
After you read	Daring Mission	108–113
Before you read	Trombones and Colleges	114–120
After you read	Trombones and Colleges	121–123
Before you read	Treasure Beneath the Sea	124–128
After you read	Treasure Beneath the Sea	129–133
After you read	Students Working: Getting the Job Done	134–136
	Words I Have Learned	137
	Words I Frequently Misspell	138
	Thoughts and Ideas From My Reading	139–140

Copyright © 1990 by Harcourt Brace Jovanovich, Inc.

All rights reserved. No part of this publication may be reproduced or transmitted in any form or by any means, electronic or mechanical, including photocopy, recording, or any information storage and retrieval system, except for the printing of complete pages, with the copyright notice, for instructional use and not for resale by any teacher using classroom quantities of the related student textbook.

Short pronunciation key and adapted entries from *HBJ School Dictionary*. Copyright © 1985 by Harcourt Brace Jovanovich, Inc. "Study Steps to Learn a Word" from *HBJ Spelling*, Signature Edition by Thorsten Carlson and Richard Madden. Copyright © 1988, 1983 by Harcourt Brace Jovanovich, Inc. Reprinted by permission of Harcourt Brace Jovanovich, Inc.

Printed in the United States of America

ISBN 0-15-329852-9

INTEREST INVENTORY

Name _____

A. Choices can be both exciting and frightening. Learning to make good choices in an important part of becoming a responsible adult. Identify how you feel about each of the following kinds of stories. This information will help you make choices about books that you may enjoy. Making choices such as these will help you become a life-long reader.

                                                                                  Circle one.

Do fantasy stories about unusual beings captivate you?	yes	no
Do you seek out stories about real people and events?	yes	no
Do you thrill to stories in which a mystery is solved?	yes	no
Are you especially interested in reading sports stories?	yes	no
Do you prefer stories about animals?	yes	no
Do stories that look like comics appeal to you?	yes	no
Do you like stories about young people just like you?	yes	no

B. Thumb through your reading book and look at some of the art. Also, look at the listing of selections on the page on the left. Answer the questions below.

1. Which selection do you most want to read? _____
   _____

2. Which selection looks like it might be funny? _____
   _____

3. Which selection might you want to read with a classmate? _____
   _____

4. Which selection might give a great deal of information? _____
   _____

INTEREST INVENTORY

Name _____

C. Read each of these sentence beginnings. Write the ending that first comes to mind. Do not worry about spelling or punctuation.

1. I think that reading is _____
   _____

2. The place and time that I most like to read is _____
   _____

3. When people read to me _____
   _____

4. When I think about going to school, I feel _____ because _____
   _____

5. My favorite subject in school is _____ because _____
   _____

6. My least favorite subject in school is _____ because _____
   _____

7. My favorite type of movie is _____
   _____

8. My favorite type of music is _____
   _____

9. My idea of a relaxing day is _____
   _____

10. I am at my best when _____
    _____

Name _____

Context clues are the other words and phrases that help you understand an unfamiliar word in a sentence.

Then the small boat vanished, and everyone on shore felt shocked that it had disappeared so suddenly.

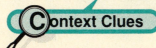

From the context clues you can find out that *vanished* means "disappeared suddenly."

Using Context Clues to Understand Unfamiliar Words

When you come to an unfamiliar word in your reading, follow these steps:

▶ Finish reading the sentence. Look for other words and phrases that help define the word.
▶ If you can't find any clues, reread the entire sentence.
▶ Use the clues to form your own definition.
▶ Read the sentence again. Substitute your definition for the word to see if it makes sense.

The vocabulary words below are from "The Race to Dog Tail Island." Knowing the words and their meanings will help you understand the story.

| collapsed | confident | current | frantically |
| gloat | gushed | thrashed | undertow |

Read each sentence. Use context clues to find the meaning of the underlined word. Then circle the letter in front of the correct meaning.

1. Jo tried not to gloat after the race, but whenever she thought about her great win she felt a great deal of delight.

   a. to win a very difficult race
   b. to think about with delight
   c. to talk about with one's best friend

STRIDES   "The Race to Dog Tail Island," pages 2–13
Vocabulary: Context Clues

Name _____

2. The swimmers were afraid that there might be an <u>undertow</u> and that the force of the water might pull them.

   a. a strong pull under the surface of the water
   b. a group of very strong swimmers
   c. a series of very high waves that crash in from the sea

3. It was easy to swim with the <u>current</u>, but turning around and swimming against the movement of the water was very difficult.

   a. a group of people who swim together
   b. a part of a body of water that is very cold
   c. a part of a body of water that moves in a certain direction

4. Leo looked <u>frantically</u> for the lost watch, but his wild search was not successful.

   a. carefully
   b. wildly
   c. in a searching way

5. Dan thought the water would just drip out of the hose, so he was surprised when the water <u>gushed</u> onto the lawn.

   a. dripped out slowly
   b. stopped flowing
   c. flowed forth suddenly

6. The little boy <u>thrashed</u> his arms for a few minutes, but soon he stopped moving them wildly and kept them at his sides.

   a. kept at one's sides
   b. moved wildly
   c. acted like a little boy

7. Roshanda usually believes she can do almost anything, and on the day of the big race she felt very <u>confident</u>.

   a. having faith in one's own abilities
   b. having unusual abilities
   c. having many good friends

8. When two other runners <u>collapsed</u> during the race, Judy helped them to their feet and held them up until they had the strength to stand by themselves.

   a. ran a good race
   b. lost a race
   c. lost strength and fell

STRIDES "The Race to Dog Tail Island," pages 2–13
Vocabulary: Context Clues

Name _____

A *synonym* is a word that has the same meaning or almost the same meaning as another word. For example, the words *sure* and *certain* have the same meaning. They are synonyms.

Read each sentence and think about the underlined word. Choose the word's synonym and write it on the line.

1. Maya was happy to leave behind the noise and rush of the city for a peaceful walk with Roy in the desert.

   A synonym for *peaceful* is _____.
   quiet   busy   sad

2. Roy leaned over the edge of the creek bed and then stepped into it, looking for fossils.

   A synonym for *leaned* is _____.
   learned   thin   bent

3. "That's dangerous," said Maya. "Haven't you ever heard of flash floods in the desert?"

   A synonym for *dangerous* is _____.
   long   weak   risky

4. Suddenly, without warning, water gushed through the creek bed.

   A synonym for *gushed* is _____.
   flowed   dripped   fell

5. Roy struggled to remain standing, but the water forced him down.

   A synonym for *struggled* is _____.
   pushed   waved   fought

6. Frantically, he reached for Maya's outstretched hand.

   A synonym for *frantically* is _____.
   wildly   happily   peacefully

7. Once he was safely on shore, Roy glanced back at the rushing water.

   A synonym for *glanced* is _____.
   smiled   looked   swam

8. Too scared to speak, he shivered at the thought of what might have happened if Maya hadn't been there to pull him to shore.

   A synonym for *scared* is _____.
   tired   afraid   calm

STRIDES "The Race to Dog Tail Island," pages 2–13
Vocabulary: Synonyms

Name _____

A writer tells a story by describing a number of events. To help the readers understand the story, the writer describes the events in the order in which they happened. In other words, the writer describes the events in *sequence*.

The map below shows how stories are organized. To identify and remember the sequence of events as you read, ask yourself questions like the ones inside the map.

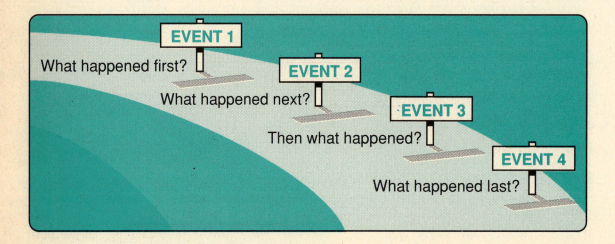

Read the paragraph about the first person to swim from England to France. As you read, use the questions to help you recognize the sequence of events.

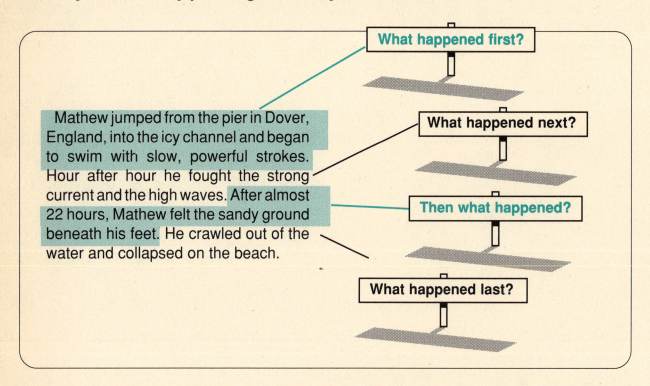

Mathew jumped from the pier in Dover, England, into the icy channel and began to swim with slow, powerful strokes. Hour after hour he fought the strong current and the high waves. After almost 22 hours, Mathew felt the sandy ground beneath his feet. He crawled out of the water and collapsed on the beach.

STRIDES "The Race to Dog Tail Island," pages 2–13
Comprehension: Sequence

Name _____

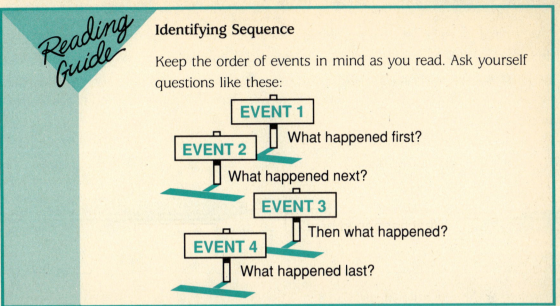

Identifying Sequence

Keep the order of events in mind as you read. Ask yourself questions like these:

- EVENT 1 — What happened first?
- EVENT 2 — What happened next?
- EVENT 3 — Then what happened?
- EVENT 4 — What happened last?

A. Read the passage. As you read, think about the sequence of events. Then read the questions and the answers.

   Jane was fixing lunch in the boat's galley when she felt a terrific jolt. A few seconds later, water began to gush through a huge hole. Jane ran up to the deck, shouting to Sallie and Fran, "Get the raft! We're sinking!" Moments later, the three friends climbed onto the little raft.

1. What happened first? _Jane felt a terrific jolt._

2. What happened next? _Water began to gush through a huge hole._

3. Then what happened? _Jane ran up to the deck and shouted to her friends._

4. What happened last? _Jane, Sallie, and Fran climbed onto the raft._

STRIDES "The Race to Dog Tail Island," pages 2–13
Comprehension: Sequence

Name _____

B. Read the passage and the questions. Write your answers on the lines.

When the race started, Ken pushed off from the edge of the pool with all his might. He kicked quickly through the water, feeling strong and confident. When he reached the far end, he pulled himself out of the water, smiling and waving to the crowd. Then, suddenly, Ken saw that two other swimmers were already there—he had not won the race after all.

1. What happened first? _____
_____
_____

2. What happened next? _____
_____
_____

3. Then what happened? _____
_____
_____

4. What happened last? _____
_____
_____

C. Think about the strategies you used to answer the questions in part B. Then read the passage and answer the questions.

Dana and her dad were loading their towels and picnic basket into the little boat when they heard the child's cries and saw his head, just barely above the water. "Help!" he called. "Help me!" Leaving their things on the beach, Dana and her father jumped into the boat and started rowing. For several minutes, they rowed silently, moving as fast as they could. Finally, they reached the tired child and grabbed his arm.

1. What happened first? _____
_____

Name _____

2. What happened next? _____
   _____
   _____

3. Then what happened? _____
   _____
   _____

4. What happened last? _____
   _____
   _____

5. Reread the passage. Use the events to fill in the sequence map.

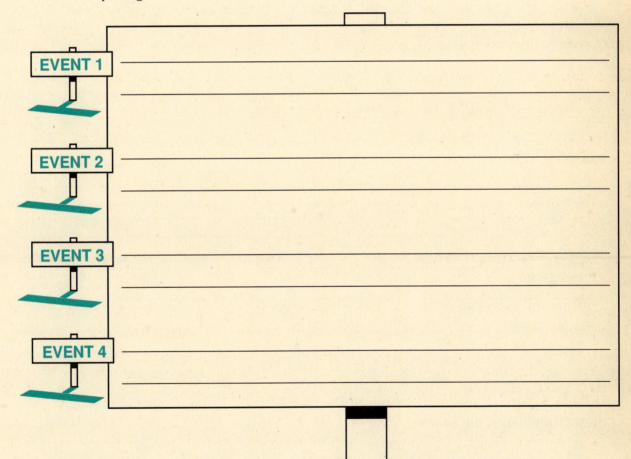

STRIDES "The Race to Dog Tail Island," pages 2–13
Comprehension: Sequence

Name _____

Remember — A writer tells a story by describing events in the order in which they happen, or in sequence.

A. Some of the events from "The Race to Dog Tail Island" are listed below. Write the events in sequence on the lines.

- The rowboat developed a leak and sank.
- Carmen walked into the lake but felt afraid to swim.
- Carmen rowed an old boat toward the island.
- Tanya tried to convince Carmen to enter the race.
- Carmen's friends started the race without her.
- Carmen decided her father's sailboat was too dangerous.

1. First, _Tanya tried to convince Carmen to enter the race._

2. Then, _____

3. Next, _____

4. Then, _____

5. Next, _____

6. Then, _____

B. What happened last in "The Race to Dog Tail Island"? Think about the ending of the story and write the answer.

_____

8   STRIDES   "The Race to Dog Tail Island," pages 2–13
Comprehension: Sequence

Name _____

Books have special parts. Every book has a title page and a copyright page. A book may also have a table of contents. A book may have a glossary, too.

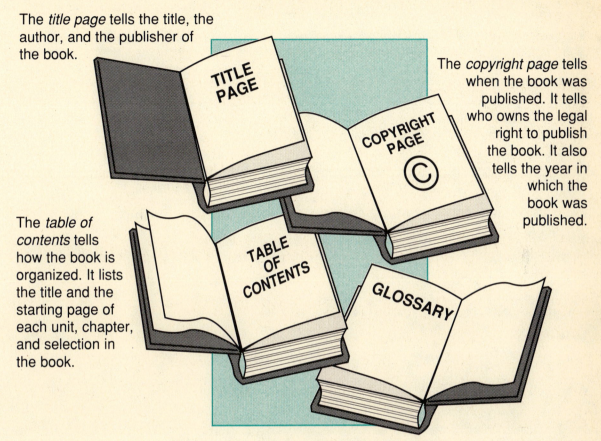

The *title page* tells the title, the author, and the publisher of the book.

The *copyright page* tells when the book was published. It tells who owns the legal right to publish the book. It also tells the year in which the book was published.

The *table of contents* tells how the book is organized. It lists the title and the starting page of each unit, chapter, and selection in the book.

The *glossary* lists the key words used in the book. It gives the meaning and pronunciation of each key word. The glossary is at the back of the book.

Read each question and all four answers. Fill in the circle with the letter of the correct answer.

1. You want to know the name of the publisher of your reading textbook. Where should you look?

    Ⓐ the title page
    Ⓑ the copyright page
    Ⓒ the table of contents
    Ⓓ the glossary

2. What is the complete title of your reading textbook?

    Ⓐ Discoveries
    Ⓑ Discoveries in Reading: Strides
    Ⓒ Harcourt Brace Jovanovich
    Ⓓ Reading

STRIDES "The Race to Dog Tail Island," pages 2–13
Study Skills: Parts of a Book

Name _____

3. What are some cities in which the publisher of your reading textbook is located?
   - (A) San Diego, Memphis, Boston
   - (B) London, Sydney, Tokyo, Paris
   - (C) Orlando, San Diego, Chicago, Dallas
   - (D) Boston, New York

4. You want to know who holds the legal right to publish your reading textbook. Where should you look?
   - (A) the title page
   - (B) the copyright page
   - (C) the table of contents
   - (D) the glossary

5. In what year was your reading textbook published?
   - (A) 1989
   - (B) 1990
   - (C) 2001
   - (D) 1952

6. You want to know how many units your reading textbook has. In which part of the book should you look?
   - (A) the title page
   - (B) the copyright page
   - (C) the table of contents
   - (D) the glossary

7. How many units does your reading textbook have?
   - (A) two
   - (B) three
   - (C) four
   - (D) five

8. What is the title of the first selection in Unit 2 of your reading textbook?
   - (A) "The Race to Dog Tail Island"
   - (B) "Sarah Tops"
   - (C) "Volcano!"
   - (D) "Daring Mission"

9. What is the title of the last selection in your reading textbook?
   - (A) "Radio Sound Effects"
   - (B) "A Night at the Ritz"
   - (C) "The Trap"
   - (D) "Getting the Job Done"

10. On what page in your reading textbook does the selection "Foreign Student" begin?
    - (A) 84
    - (B) 55
    - (C) 86
    - (D) 115

11. You want to know the meaning of a difficult word in your reading textbook. Where should you look?
    - (A) the title page
    - (B) the copyright page
    - (C) the table of contents
    - (D) the glossary

12. On what page in your reading textbook does the glossary begin?
    - (A) 1
    - (B) 55
    - (C) 214
    - (D) 228

STRIDES   "The Race to Dog Tail Island," pages 2–13
Study Skills: Parts of a Book

Name _____

Fiction and nonfiction are two different kinds of writing.

In *fiction*, the setting, events, or characters are made up by the writer. Part of the story may be based on facts, but fiction always includes at least some made-up information. One example of fiction is a book of stories about a made-up person who likes to play baseball.

Nonfiction tells about facts. The setting, events, and people in nonfiction are all real. One example of nonfiction is a book about the lives of real baseball players.

Read these items. Each one describes a book. Write your answers to the questions.

1. A book about the life of a famous dancer

    a. Is it fiction or nonfiction? _____

    b. How do you know? _____

2. A book of true stories about real students at a real school

    a. Is it fiction or nonfiction? _____

    b. How do you know? _____

3. A book of stories about talking animals

    a. Is it fiction or nonfiction? _____

    b. How do you know? _____

4. A book of interesting facts about soccer

    a. Is it fiction or nonfiction? _____

    b. How do you know? _____

5. A book of stories about made-up events in a real setting

    a. Is it fiction or nonfiction? _____

    b. How do you know? _____

6. A book about the history of airplanes

    a. Is it fiction or nonfiction? _____

    b. How do you know? _____

STRIDES "The Race to Dog Tail Island," pages 2–13
Literature: Fiction/Nonfiction

Name _____

Scanning is a special way of reading to find information quickly. When you need to find a word or an idea on a page but do not need to read the entire page for meaning, you should scan. For example, you may need to scan to find a specific vocabulary word or to answer a specific question.

> **Reading Guide**
>
> **Scanning for Information**
> To scan for information, follow these steps:
>
> ▶ Identify a key word or phrase.
> ▶ Keep the key word or phrase in your mind.
> ▶ Look over each line of print very quickly. Do not stop until you see your key word or phrase.
> ▶ Read the sentence or paragraph that includes your key word or phrase. Check to see that you found the correct information.

Scan each set of paragraphs below. Find the key word or name identified in the directions.

1. Scan these paragraphs. Find and circle the word *earthquake*.

    The game was nearly over when it happened. At first, Louis thought the movement was coming from the stomping of the fans' feet. Then he noticed the goal posts swaying back and forth.
    On the playing field, the men in uniform seemed confused. The ball was out of play, and the players were glancing into the stands.
    Suddenly, a voice came over the loudspeakers. "Ladies and gentlemen," it said, "We are experiencing a minor earthquake. Please remain seated until it passes."

2. Scan these paragraphs. Find and circle the name of the stadium. Hint: Before you begin, think about what will make the name easy to spot.

    Louis had only been in California for one week. "So this is what earthquakes are like," he thought. A wavy feeling ran through his head. A low growl seemed to come from deep down under the ground.
    Gradually the dizziness in Louis's head stopped. He looked around. The benches at Anaheim Stadium were no longer moving. On the field, the goal posts had stopped swaying.

3. Scan the paragraphs again. Find and circle the word *growl*.

STRIDES   "The Pride of Madison High," pages 14–25
Study Skills: Scanning

Name _____

Context clues are the other words and phrases that help you understand an unfamiliar word in a sentence. Sometimes you have to read more than one sentence to find context clues.

Josh was a very aggressive football player. He always played each game with great energy, and fought hard to win each point.

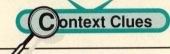

From the context clues you can find out that *aggressive* means "energetic and hard-fighting."

Reading Guide

Using Context Clues to Understand Unfamiliar Words
When you come to an unfamiliar word in your reading, follow these steps:

▶ Finish reading the paragraph in which you found the unfamiliar word, and look for context clues.
▶ If you don't find good clues, reread the sentences before the one with the unfamiliar word, and look for context clues there.
▶ Use the clues to form your own definition.
▶ Reread the sentence with the unfamiliar word. Substitute your definition for the word to see if it makes sense.

The vocabulary words below are from "The Pride of Madison High." Knowing the words and their meanings will help you understand the story.

> artificial   autograph   ceremony   disbelief
> graduated   handicapped   inspired

A. Follow the directions to find each of these words in the selection. Then use context clues to find the meaning of the word. Circle the letter in front of the best definition.

1. Scan page 17 to find the word *inspired*. In the paragraph, *inspired* means _____.
   a. filled with feelings of anger
   b. strong and powerful
   c. filled with a desire to do something

STRIDES   "The Pride of Madison High," pages 14–25
Vocabulary: Context Clues

Before you read

Name _____

2. Scan page 18 to find the word *artificial*. In the paragraph, *artificial* means _____.
   a. made by people
   b. natural
   c. ancient

3. Scan page 20 to find the word *handicapped*. In the paragraph, *handicapped* means _____.
   a. a good golf player
   b. unable to do certain things because of a physical problem
   c. pleasing in the way one looks

4. Scan page 22 to find the word *ceremony*. In the paragraph, *ceremony* means _____.
   a. a series of formal actions performed on a special occasion
   b. an indoor game
   c. a gathering of people to discuss new laws

B. Read each paragraph. Use context clues to figure out the meaning of the underlined word. Circle the letter in front of the best definition.

1. Jerry's grandparents had not been able to go to high school. His mother and father had both spent a few years in high school, but neither of them had finished. Jerry's younger brother Ben is just starting high school. Jerry is the first member of his family who has ever been <u>graduated</u> from high school.

   a. started studying
   b. finished a course of study
   c. considered very smart and talented

2. Lori handed the book to her friend. She laughed and said, "Be sure you write your name here. I want to have your <u>autograph</u>."

   a. a person's complete name
   b. a sample of a person's best handwriting
   c. a person's name written in that person's own handwriting

3. Marla shook her head in <u>disbelief</u>. She wanted to think that her brother's story was true, but it just didn't seem possible.

   a. a thought or feeling that something is untrue
   b. a thought or feeling that something must be true
   c. a thought or feeling that all people are friendly

STRIDES "The Pride of Madison High," pages 14–25
Vocabulary: Context Clues

Name _____

A *compound word* is one word formed by joining two words. Often, you can guess the meaning of a compound word by thinking about the meanings of the two smaller words. For example, *sidelines* are the *lines* at the *side* of a playing field.

Underline the compound word in each sentence. Think about the meaning of each of the two smaller words in the compound word. Then circle the letter in front of the best definition of the compound word.

1. Molly is a successful journalist who writes for many newspapers.
    a. papers that have not been used before
    b. people who publish storybooks
    c. papers that tell the news

2. Although she says anyone can write as well as she does, Molly has actually worked very hard to refine her skills.
    a. any person   b. all young people   c. any trained writer

3. Molly prefers writing about sports, especially women's basketball.
    a. a hobby of making baskets
    b. a game played with a basket and a ball
    c. a game played with many different balls

4. Her coverage of youth football in America earned her a nomination for a Pulitzer Prize.
    a. a game in which only one player can touch the ball
    b. a game in which all the players must stay on their feet
    c. a game in which a player can use his or her foot to kick the ball

5. Recently, she has been writing about boating contests such as the sailboat competitions in the Gulf of Mexico.
    a. a boat that is for sale   b. a boat with a sail   c. a boat not costing much

6. To report on one event, she sat in a tiny rowboat with a camera and a writing pad.
    a. a boat that people move by rowing
    b. a boat that belongs in a line
    c. a boat made for swimmers

7. Fortunately the boat was watertight, because Molly does not know how to swim.
    a. too tight to fit comfortably
    b. so tight that air cannot leak out
    c. so tight that water cannot leak in

STRIDES "The Pride of Madison High," pages 14–25
Vocabulary: Compound Words

 **Before you read**

Name _____

A *conclusion* is a judgment reached by logical thinking. As you read a selection, you draw conclusions about the main character. You think about what the character is like, and you draw conclusions about the character's most important qualities, or traits.

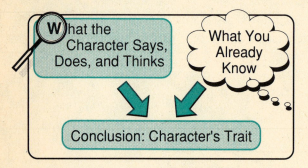

In most stories, the writer does not directly state the character's traits. Instead, the writer shows the traits by describing what the character says, does, and thinks. You can use that information in the story, along with what you already know, to draw conclusions about the character's traits.

What character trait does Ann have?

　　Ann reaches out to silence the buzzing alarm. In the darkness, the numbers on her clock glow—5:30. She dresses quickly and goes downstairs. There she turns on the heat, puts the clean dishes away, and sets the table for breakfast. Ann hums to herself as she puts on her jacket, grabs her carrying bag, and heads out the back door.
　　Ann goes directly to the covered box at the corner. Mr. Kelly always leaves the newspapers there. She yanks the box open, loads her carrier, and sets off on her route.

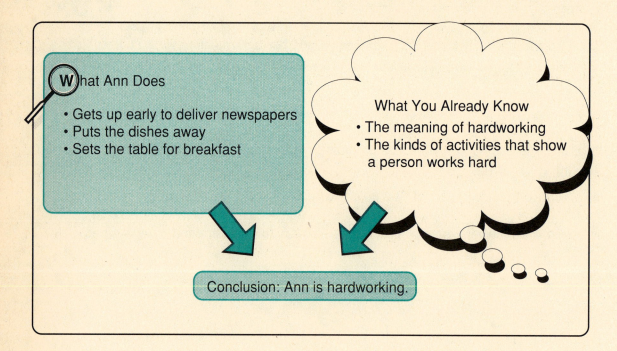

STRIDES　"The Pride of Madison High," pages 14–25
Comprehension:　Conclusions

Name _____

Reading Guide

Drawing Conclusions About Character Traits

As you read about characters follow these steps:

▶ Look for things the characters do, say, or think that show their traits.

▶ Think about what you already know about people and how they act.

▶ Combine the information about the characters with what you already know to draw a conclusion.

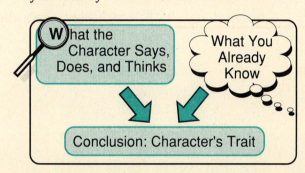

Here are some common character traits.

kindness	shyness	thoughtfulness	confidence
ambition	trustworthiness	determination	friendliness

A. Read the passage about Ann. As you read, think about what she does, says, and thinks. Then read the question and the answers.

    As Ann delivers the papers, she stops herself from thinking about how much she'd rather be back home in bed, warm and dreaming. Instead she thinks about going to State College in a few years. The money she earns now will help pay her expenses. After college, Ann plans to be a reporter. She wants to write news stories for the paper she is delivering now.

Ann is *ambitious*. What does she *think* and *do* to show this trait? Circle the letters in front of three answers.

ⓐ She wants to go to college.
b. She wishes she were back home in bed.
ⓒ She is earning money to help pay her college expenses.
ⓓ She wants to be a newspaper reporter.

STRIDES "The Pride of Madison High," pages 14–25
Comprehension: Conclusions

17

Name _____

B. Read the passage about Dirk. Then follow the directions to answer the question.

   Dirk races to the bus stop and arrives just as the school bus pulls up. He climbs aboard the bus, smiles at the driver, and says "Good morning." He sits down next to his friend Will, and the two begin talking. At the next stop, a boy whom Dirk has never seen before gets on the bus and sits in the seat behind him.

   Dirk turns around. "Hi," he says. "I'm Dirk Waters, and this is my friend Will Hirami. You must be new."

   "Yes, we just moved here. I'm Jess Molina," he answers.

   "Great! When we get to school, Will and I will show you around. We can meet you for lunch, too. We usually eat with a big group of kids—I'm sure you'll like them," Dirk explains.

Dirk is *friendly*. What does he *say* and *do* to show this trait? Circle the letters in front of two answers.

a. He runs to the bus stop.
b. He says "Good morning" to the driver.
c. He sits down on the bus.
d. He introduces himself to the new boy.

C. Think about the strategies you used to answer the question in part B. Then read the passage and answer the question.

   At the end of the rehearsal, Ms. Wilkins calls everyone together. "Renee and Lou were supposed to clean up today," she tells the students, "but they're both sick. I'm afraid I'll have to ask someone else to help." She looks around the stage. "What about you, Jill?"

   "Sure," says Jill. "I don't mind cleaning up this time." Jill's friends gather their books and jackets and head for the door. Jill smiles and calls to them, "Bye. See you tomorrow."

   Jill gets right to work. She hangs up the costumes on the rack. Then she organizes the props neatly on a long row of shelves. As she works, she hums a happy tune from the show they have been rehearsing.

   Ms. Wilkins helps Jill move a heavy table off the stage. "I guess that's all, Jill. Thanks so much for staying," she says. "You really did a great job!"

Jill is *cheerful*. What does she *say* and *do* to show this trait? Circle the letters in front of three answers.

a. She tells Ms. Wilkins that she doesn't mind helping.
b. She smiles at her friends as they leave.
c. She does a good job of organizing all the props.
d. She hums happily while she works.

STRIDES "The Pride of Madison High," pages 14–25
Comprehension: Conclusions

Name _____

You can use information in the selection, along with what you already know, to draw conclusions about a character.

In "The Pride of Madison High," Carl Joseph has traits that help him overcome his handicap. Read each question. Think about what Carl says, does, and thinks to show the trait. Then circle the letter in front of the answer or answers, or write your answers on the lines.

1. Carl is courageous. What does he *do* to show this trait? Circle two.
   a. He has many friends.
   b. He plays football even though he has only one leg.
   c. He fights when other students tease him about being crippled.
   d. He never feels sorry for himself.

2. Carl is confident. What does he *say* and *do* to show this trait? Circle two.
   a. He says he never worries that he can't do something; he just goes out and does it.
   b. He is shocked when he finds out about the Carl Joseph Appreciation Day celebration.
   c. He plays several sports and runs for vice president of the student body.
   d. He tells reporters that he is proud of playing on his high school football, basketball, and track teams.

3. Carl is a talented athlete. What does he *do* to show this trait? Circle two.
   a. He has served as the vice president of the student body for four years.
   b. He never feels sorry for himself.
   c. In one football game, he hops down the field and tackles the other team's quarterback.
   d. He clears 5'10" in the high jump.

4. Carl is ambitious. You can conclude that Carl has this trait because he has two goals. What are these goals?

   a. _____
   _____

   b. _____
   _____

STRIDES "The Pride of Madison High," pages 14–25
Comprehension: Conclusions

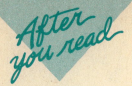

Name _____

A good news story usually begins with a lead paragraph. The *lead paragraph* gives the readers the most important facts of the story in just a few sentences. The sentences of a lead paragraph should tell *who, what, when, where,* and *why.*

Read the lead paragraph for this news story. Then read the list of facts that tell *who, what, when, where,* and *why.*

JOSEPH ELECTED FOR FOURTH YEAR

Carl Joseph was elected yesterday to be the vice president of the Madison High student body for this year. Joseph, a senior, is well liked and admired by Madison students. This is the fourth year he has been elected the school's student body vice president.

Who: Carl Joseph
What: elected vice president of the student body
When: yesterday
Where: Madison High
Why: because he is well liked and admired

Read this list of facts. Use the facts to write the first two sentences of the lead paragraph for a news story about an event from "The Pride of Madison High." Use other facts from the story to write one more sentence about what happened.

Who: the people of Madison
What: held a Carl Joseph Appreciation Day
When: last Saturday night
Where: Madison High School
Why: to honor Carl and to let others know about his accomplishments

_____
_____
_____
_____
_____
_____

STRIDES "The Pride of Madison High," pages 14–25
Language: News Story

Name _____

You can use a *glossary* to check the definition, spelling, and pronunciation of the key words in a book. The words in a glossary are arranged in alphabetical order. By using alphabetical order, you can find a glossary entry quickly and easily.

A. Write the words from each box in alphabetical order.

1. necessary _____
   narrator _____
   number _____
   nickel _____
   notice _____

2. initials _____
   ideal _____
   item _____
   ivory _____
   island _____

3. conductor _____
   country _____
   costume _____
   cotton _____
   collect _____

4. director _____
   diagram _____
   digit _____
   discus _____
   differ _____

5. express _____
   export _____
   expand _____
   expect _____
   explain _____

6. compartment _____
   comedy _____
   comic _____
   combine _____
   comma _____

STRIDES "The Four-Fifteen Express," pages 28–43
Vocabulary: Glossary

Name _____

B. Study the sample glossary entry. Read the notes about each part of the entry. Then write the answers to the questions.

- The *entry word* is in dark type. This is the word for which information is given.
- The *pronunciation* shows how the word is said. A *pronunciation* key in the glossary explains which sound each letter stands for.
- An abbreviation in italics tells the *part of speech*. For example, *v.* stands for *verb*, and *n.* stands for *noun*.
- The *definition* tells what the word means.
- Other *forms* of the entry word are given in dark type.

en·grave [in·grāv'] *v.* **en·graved, en·graving** To carve or cut letters or designs into: Mom and Dad asked the jeweler to *engrave* their rings. *syn.* carve

- The *example sentence* shows how the word can be used.
- If the entry word has a *synonym*, it is shown at the end of the glossary entry.

1. What is the entry word in the sample glossary entry? _____

2. What two other forms of that word are given? _____

3. What does the pronunciation in a glossary entry tell you? _____
_____

4. What does the letter *v.* in the sample tell you about the word *engrave*? _____
_____

5. What does *engrave* mean? _____
_____

6. Use the word *engrave* in a sentence of your own to show that you understand its meaning.
_____

22

STRIDES "The Four-Fifteen Express," pages 28–43
Vocabulary: Glossary

Name _____

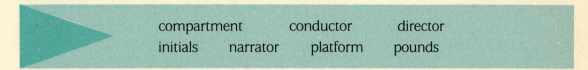

The vocabulary words below are from "The Four-Fifteen Express." Knowing the words and their meanings will help you understand the story.

> compartment   conductor   director
> initials   narrator   platform   pounds

Read each word. Look the word up in the glossary of your textbook, and write the definition. Then complete the sentence. Your sentence should show that you understand the word's meaning.

1. **compartment**

   a. In the glossary, *compartment* means _____
   _____
   _____.

   b. We were surprised to find that the *compartment* was _____
   _____.

2. **conductor**

   a. In the glossary, *conductor* means _____
   _____
   _____.

   b. The *conductor* stopped each passenger and _____
   _____.

3. **director**

   a. In the glossary, *director* means _____
   _____
   _____.

   b. The *director* of the company should _____
   _____.

STRIDES   "The Four-Fifteen Express," pages 28–43
Vocabulary: Word Meanings

Before you read

Name _____

4. **initials**

   a. In the glossary, *initials* means _____
   _____
   _____.

   b. These *initials* on the contract show that _____
   _____.

5. **narrator**

   a. In the glossary, *narrator* means _____
   _____
   _____.

   b. We didn't understand the story because the *narrator* _____
   _____.

6. **platform**

   a. In the glossary, *platform* means _____
   _____
   _____.

   b. The people on the *platform* were all _____
   _____.

7. **pounds**

   a. In the glossary, *pounds* means _____
   _____
   _____.

   b. If we had five more *pounds,* we would be able to _____
   _____.

STRIDES "The Four-Fifteen Express," pages 28–43
Vocabulary: Word Meanings

Name _____

Before you read

Many words have more than one meaning. You may notice a word with *multiple meanings* in your reading. You can use context clues to figure out which meaning the writer has used.

Each of these words has multiple meanings. Match each sentence with the correct meaning. Write the letter of the correct meaning on the line in front of the sentence.

1. **pounds**
   - **a.** strikes or hits
   - **b.** units of weight
   - **c.** units of money

   _____ How many pounds does your cat weigh?

   _____ In England your book would cost two pounds.

   _____ The butcher pounds some cuts of meat to make them tender.

2. **conductor**
   - **a.** someone who leads a musical group
   - **b.** someone who collects tickets on a train
   - **c.** something heat or electricity runs through

   _____ The conductor took our tickets as we boarded the train.

   _____ The band just hired a new conductor.

   _____ Metal is a good conductor of heat.

3. **express**
   - **a.** to tell in words
   - **b.** a fast train or bus that makes few stops
   - **c.** to send by rapid delivery

   _____ The store will express the package to you today.

   _____ Jeff could hardly find the words to express his thanks.

   _____ We'll spend less time on the train if we wait for the noon express.

4. **line**
   - **a.** to form a row
   - **b.** a route for trains or buses
   - **c.** a slender mark

   _____ Someone had drawn a red line through my notes.

   _____ The bus company plans to add a new line next year.

   _____ The teacher asked the children to line up at the door.

STRIDES "The Four-Fifteen Express," pages 28–43
Vocabulary: Multiple Meanings

After you read

Name _____

Remember The sequence of events is the order in which the events happen.

Read the list of seven important events from "The Four-Fifteen Express." Write the events in sequence on the lines. One event has already been written in it's correct place.

Julia and Penelope question Raikes.
Penelope and Derry meet and talk on the train.
Raikes admits that he killed Derry.
Derry leaves the train in Blackwater.
Penelope and Julia question the conductor and the guard.
Penelope jumps off the train.
Penelope tells Julia about meeting Derry on the train.

1. _____

2. _____

3. _____

4. _____

5. *Penelope and Julia question the conductor and the guard.*

6. _____

7. _____

Name _____

Dialogue is the conversation between characters in a story or a play. In a play, much of the action is described through dialogue. Understanding dialogue will help you understand the action in a play.

Read each paragraph. Then rewrite it as part of a play. Use dialogue to tell the story. The first line of dialogue has already been written.

Janet wants to go to Fresno. She is at the ticket counter of the train station. Janet wants to know the price of a ticket to Fresno. The ticket agent tells her that the price is $17.50. She also wants to know what time the train leaves. The ticket agent tells her that a train for Fresno leaves at 10:15 every morning. Janet buys a ticket.

Ticket Agent: *Can I help you?* _____

Janet: _____

Ticket Agent: _____

Janet: _____

Ticket Agent: _____

Janet: _____

Janet is on the train. She asks the conductor the way to the dining car. The conductor tells Janet that the dining car is four cars back. She also asks him when lunch is served. He tells her that lunch is served from 11:30 A.M. until 2:00 P.M.

Janet: _____

Conductor: _____

Janet: _____

Conductor: _____

STRIDES "The Four-Fifteen Express," pages 28–43
Language: Dialogue

Before you read

Name _____

When you find the *main idea* of a passage, you identify the most important information the writer presents.

Study the map, the sidenotes, and the example. The map shows how the paragraph is organized.

The *topic* of a paragraph is it's subject. It is a word or phrase that tells what the paragraph is generally about. To identify the topic, ask yourself: What is this paragraph about?

The *main idea* of a paragraph is the most important sentence that explains the topic. To find the main idea, ask yourself: What sentence states the most important idea about the subject or topic?

Supporting details are all other sentences in the paragraph that explain or tell about the main idea.

Radio News

The development of radio broadcasting provided a way for people to learn about news soon after it happened. Until radio broadcasting became popular in the 1920's, there was no way for people to hear about events in other parts of the world until long after they happened. Radio brought up-to-date news right into people's homes.

STRIDES   "Radio Sound Effects," pages 44–51
Comprehension: Topics and Stated Main Ideas of Paragraphs

Name _____

Before you read

Reading Guide

Identifying the Main Idea of a Paragraph

As you read a paragraph, follow these steps to look for the main idea:

▶ First find the topic. Ask: What is this paragraph about?
▶ Find the main idea. Look for the sentence that tells the most important idea about the topic.

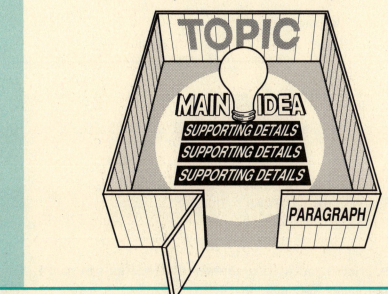

A. As you read the paragraph, look for the main idea. Then read the questions and the answers.

"Dragnet" was a popular radio show during the 1950's. It was a drama telling how a pair of police officers solved crimes. Each week Sergeant Joe Friday and his partner tracked down and arrested a person who had broken the law. Realistic sound effects, exciting situations, and Jack Webb's acting in the role of Sergeant Friday made the show popular.

1. **TOPIC** What is the paragraph about? Circle one.
   a. home entertainment
   (b.) "Dragnet"
   c. solving crimes
   d. famous actors

2. **MAIN IDEA** Which sentence states the most important idea about the topic? _____
   "Dragnet" was a popular radio show during the 1950's.

3. Where in the paragraph is the main idea sentence? _It is the first sentence of the paragraph._

STRIDES "Radio Sound Effects," pages 44–51
Comprehension: Topics and Stated Main Ideas of Paragraphs

Name _____

B. **Read the paragraph. Circle the letter in front of the answer, or write your answers on the lines.**

Early radios were strange-looking pieces of equipment. The crystal radio, used in the early 1920's, was an open box with wires plugged into it. It didn't need batteries, but it could be heard only with earphones. An electric radio of the middle 1920's had a loudspeaker mounted to the top. Later radios of the 1930's and 1940's were heavy and boxy with large dials on the front.

1. TOPIC   What is the paragraph about?
   a. the crystal radio
   b. listening to the radio
   c. earphones
   d. what old radios looked like

2. MAIN IDEA   Which sentence states the most important idea about the topic? _____
   _____
   _____

3. Where in the paragraph is the main idea sentence? _____
   _____

C. **Think about the strategies you used to answer the questions in part B. Then read the paragraph and answer the questions.**

Comedy shows were extremely popular during radio's Golden Age. Jack Benny was one of radio's top comedians, and his show drew a large audience. George Burns and Gracie Allen were a popular husband-and-wife comedy team whose show made thousands of people laugh. During the grim years of World War II, comedy shows on the radio brought cheer to listeners across the country.

1. TOPIC   What is the paragraph about?
   a. Jack Benny
   b. how to make people laugh
   c. World War II
   d. radio comedies

2. MAIN IDEA   Which sentence states the most important idea about the topic? _____
   _____
   _____

3. Where in the paragraph is the main idea sentence? _____
   _____

Name _____

D. Read the paragraph below. Then fill in the map.

Radio is still popular today in spite of the growth of television. One reason for this is that listeners can always hear music on the radio. When radio stations began broadcasting rock music in the 1950's, they gained many listeners, especially young people. Another reason for radio's popularity is that news is broadcast often. The invention of small radios that can easily be carried from place to place has also helped keep radio popular.

TOPIC

_____
_____

MAIN IDEA

_____
_____
_____

SUPPORTING DETAILS

1. _____
_____
_____

2. _____
_____
_____

3. _____
_____
_____

4. _____
_____
_____

Name _____

 The *topic* of a paragraph is its subject. The *main idea* is the most important idea about the topic. Each paragraph may have a main idea. The other sentences in the paragraph explain or tell about the main idea. They give *supporting details*.

A. Read paragraph 3 that begins on page 46 of "Radio Sound Effects." Then answer the questions below. For question 1, circle the letter in front of the correct answer. For question 2, write the answer on the lines.

1. **TOPIC** What is the paragraph about?
   a. thunderstorms
   b. making loud noises
   c. using sounds to make pictures in the mind
   d. city noises

2. **MAIN IDEA** What sentence states the most important idea about the topic? _____

_____

_____

_____

B. Read paragraph 1 on page 47 of "Radio Sound Effects." Then answer the questions below. For question 1, circle the letter in front of the correct answer. For question 2, write the answer on the lines.

1. **TOPIC** What is the paragraph about?
   a. Arch Oboler's sound effects
   b. giant earthworms
   c. scary movies
   d. stories that are hard to believe

2. **MAIN IDEA** What sentence states the most important idea about the topic? _____

_____

_____

_____

STRIDES "Radio Sound Effects," pages 44–51
Comprehension: Topics and Stated Main Ideas of Paragraphs

Name _____

C. Read the last paragraph on page 47 of "Radio Sound Effects."
   Then fill in the map.

TOPIC
_____
_____
_____

MAIN IDEA
_____
_____
_____
_____

SUPPORTING DETAILS

1. _____
   _____
   _____
   _____

2. _____
   _____
   _____
   _____

3. _____
   _____
   _____
   _____

STRIDES "Radio Sound Effects," pages 44–51
Comprehension: Topics and Stated Main Ideas of Paragraphs

Name _____

Everyone wants to get good scores on tests. Following directions is an important part of doing well on any kind of test. Read all test directions carefully. Key words in the directions will help you mark your answers correctly.

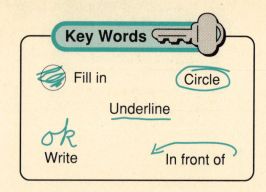

Matthew and Jennifer marked answers to some questions about "Radio Sound Effects." Notice how well each student followed the directions.

▶ Which student really followed the directions?
▶ Which student did not read all of the directions? What happened to this student's work?

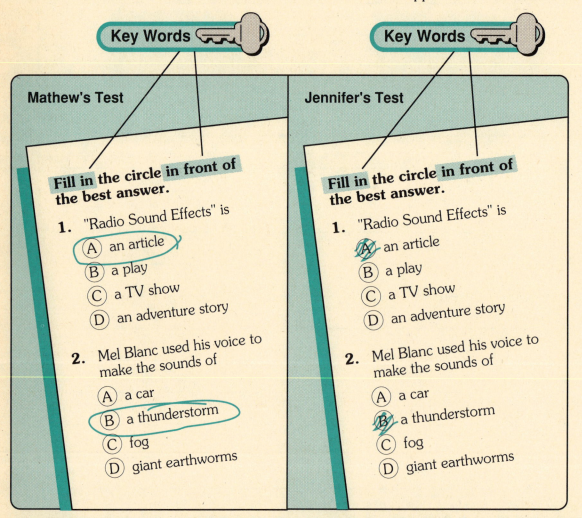

STRIDES "Radio Sound Effects," pages 44–51
Study Skills: Test-Taking Strategies

Name _____

Reading Guide

Using Test-Taking Strategies

Follow these steps when taking a test:

▶ Read the directions carefully.
▶ Look for key words in the directions such as
  fill in,
  circle,
  and *underline.*

Read each sentence. Fill in the circle in front of the best answer.

1. Everyone wants to get _____ on tests.
   Ⓐ good scores
   Ⓑ low scores
   Ⓒ wrong answers
   Ⓓ through quickly

2. _____ is an important part of doing well on any kind of test.
   Ⓐ Hurrying
   Ⓑ Worrying
   Ⓒ Following directions
   Ⓓ Writing

3. Read _____ test directions carefully.
   Ⓐ all
   Ⓑ the first
   Ⓒ the important
   Ⓓ some

4. _____ in the directions will help you mark your answers correctly.
   Ⓐ Answers
   Ⓑ Key words
   Ⓒ Punctuation
   Ⓓ Capital letters

5. Jennifer _____ directions carefully.
   Ⓐ did not follow
   Ⓑ followed
   Ⓒ wrote
   Ⓓ underlined

STRIDES "Radio Sound Effects," pages 44–51
Study Skills: Test-Taking Strategies

Name _____

The vocabulary words below are from "Sarah Tops." Knowing the words and their meanings will help you understand the story.

> conscience   directory   loomed
> snout   twilight

Read each word and its definition. Then circle the letter in front of the correct answer.

1. **conscience:** the inner understanding that tells a person if an action is right or wrong.

   _____ is likely to cause a person to have a guilty conscience.

   a. Going to school
   b. Sharing a sandwich
   c. Hurting a friend's feelings
   d. Writing a book report

2. **directory:** a list of names and addresses in alphabetical order.

   _____ can be found in a telephone directory.

   a. A list of library books
   b. The school's phone number
   c. The football scores
   d. Directions for baking bread

3. **loomed:** appeared unclearly but seemed large or threatening.

   If a bear loomed in the darkness of the forest, a hiker could _____.

   a. hear it but not see it
   b. touch it before seeing it
   c. see it very clearly
   d. see it, but not very clearly

4. **snout:** the forward part of the head of many animals, usually including the nose and jaws.

   A pig's snout would never be used for _____.

   a. digging
   b. smelling
   c. chewing
   d. hearing

5. **twilight:** the light in the sky just after sunset or just before sunrise.

   I can just see the hill in the twilight soon after _____.

   a. the sun goes down
   b. the sun comes up
   c. it is completely dark
   d. everyone goes to sleep

STRIDES "Sarah Tops," pages 54–63
Vocabulary: Word Meanings

Name _____

A *synonym* is a word that has the same or almost the same meaning as another word. *Snout* and *nose* are synonyms. Paying attention to which synonym is used will help a reader understand the writer's exact meaning.

The words in each box below are synonyms. Follow the directions to arrange each group of words in a special order. The lists can be arranged in more than one way. Be ready to explain why you chose the order you did. Share your lists with your classmates. Discuss how the lists are alike and different.

1.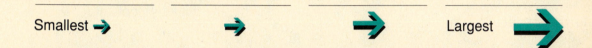

   giant   large   huge   enormous

   These synonyms show size. Write the words in order from smallest to largest.

   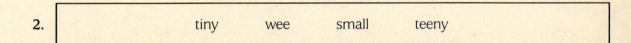

   Smallest → _____ → _____ → _____ Largest → _____

2.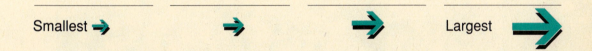

   tiny   wee   small   teeny

   These synonyms show size. Write the words in order from smallest to largest.

   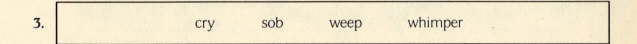

   Smallest → _____ → _____ → _____ Largest → _____

3.

   cry   sob   weep   whimper

   These synonyms show sadness. Write the words in order from the one that shows the least sadness to the one that shows the most.

   Least ▭ _____   _____   _____   Most ▭ _____

STRIDES "Sarah Tops," pages 54–63
Vocabulary: Synonyms

Name _____

Writers use both facts and opinions when they write.

 **Fact**
Something that can be proved.

Opinion
Something that someone believes, thinks, or feels but cannot prove.

To distinguish between facts and opinions, ask yourself this question:
Can this statement be proved?

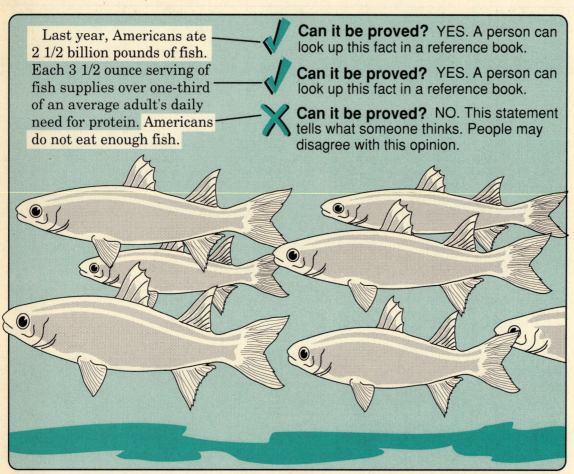

Last year, Americans ate 2 1/2 billion pounds of fish. — **Can it be proved?** YES. A person can look up this fact in a reference book.

Each 3 1/2 ounce serving of fish supplies over one-third of an average adult's daily need for protein. — **Can it be proved?** YES. A person can look up this fact in a reference book.

Americans do not eat enough fish. — **Can it be proved?** NO. This statement tells what someone thinks. People may disagree with this opinion.

Below are some words and phrases writers often use in opinion statements.

I think	beautiful	fun	interesting
enjoyable	better	best	worst
maybe	I believe	Some people think	
Some people believe		In my opinion	

STRIDES "Sarah Tops," pages 54–63
Comprehension: Facts and Opinions

Name _____

Reading Guide

Distinguishing Facts from Opinions
To identify facts and opinions, follow these steps:

▶ Look for words and phrases that signal an opinion statement.
▶ Ask yourself: *Can this statement be proved, or is it what someone thinks?*

A. Read each paragraph. Think about whether each statement in the paragraph can be proved. Then read the questions and the answers.

1. If they were straightened out, the threads of some spiders' webs would be more than 300 miles long. Spider webs look and feel awful. Nevertheless, people should not destroy spider webs.

   a. Which statement is a fact? _the first_

   b. How do you know? _It can be proved. A person can look it up in a reference book._

2. Swifts are the fastest-flying birds in the world. I think they are interesting to watch and study. They eat flying insects, which they catch in mid-flight.

   a. Which statement is an opinion? _the second_

   b. How do you know? _It cannot be proved. It tells what someone thinks._

Name _____

B. Read each paragraph. Then read the questions and write your answers on the lines.

1. Whales are extremely beautiful animals. They are the largest animals ever to live on the planet, larger even than the biggest dinosaur. Even so, they can jump high into the air.

   a. Which statement is an opinion? _____

   b. How do you know? _____
   _____

2. I think coral reefs house some of the most unusual animals ever seen. The strawberry sponge is one animal that lives on a coral reef. It is fun to read about strange animals like sponges.

   a. Which statement is a fact? _____

   b. How do you know? _____
   _____

C. Think about the strategies you used to answer the questions in part B. Then read each paragraph and answer the questions.

1. Of the 300 types of sharks, 5 are known to harm humans. Most sharks live in saltwater, but some live in freshwater lakes. Sharks are ugly animals.

   a. Which statement is an opinion? _____

   b. How do you know? _____
   _____

2. The blue-striped angelfish is the prettiest fish in the ocean. In the wild, the angelfish's colors hide it from enemies. My angelfish prefers living in my aquarium, where she is safe.

   a. Which statement is a fact? _____

   b. How do you know? _____
   _____

3. Yellowfin tuna often swim under schools of dolphins. Often dolphins are caught and die in the nets with the tuna. For this reason, I believe people should not eat tuna.

   a. Which statement is an opinion? _____

   b. How do you know? _____
   _____

40 STRIDES "Sarah Tops," pages 54–63
Comprehension: Facts and Opinions

Name _____

Remember A *fact* can be proved to be true. An *opinion* is what someone believes, thinks, or feels but cannot prove about a subject.

In a mystery story like "Sarah Tops," the reader can arrive at the solution by deciding what information is fact and what is opinion.

Read each sentence from "Sarah Tops." Write *F* in front of the sentence if it is a *fact*. Write *O* in front of the sentence if it is an *opinion*. Reread parts of the story, if necessary.

_____ 1. My Dad is a detective for the police.

_____ 2. "A man leaving the museum was killed," Dad answered.

_____ 3. "They caught up with him outside, killed him, and ran off."

_____ 4. "One diamond is still missing."

_____ 5. "Maybe that's what the killers were after," I said.

_____ 6. "The dead man may have been trying to double-cross the other two."

_____ 7. "Maybe the dead man left it with Sarah Tops, whoever she is."

_____ 8. "There's no Sarah Tops in the city directory, either with one P or with two P's."

_____ 9. "Maybe Sarah Tops isn't a person," I said. "Maybe it's a company. . . ."

_____ 10. "Maybe the dead man has a daughter named Sarah. Maybe he cut a hole in her toy top and hid the diamond inside and . . . ."

_____ 11. "But the dead man doesn't have a daughter named Sarah."

_____ 12. It was a wonderful skeleton.

_____ 13. It had two horns over the eyes.

_____ 14. The nameplate said *Triceratops*.

STRIDES "Sarah Tops," pages 54–63
Comprehension: Facts and Opinions

Name _____

Advertisements may contain both facts and opinions. Some advertisements may try to lead you to think a certain way by giving opinions. To make good decisions about what to buy, decide which statements are facts and which are opinions. Then base your decisions on the facts, not on the opinions.

Read each advertisement below. Decide which statements are facts and which ones are opinions. Then follow the directions.

1. Underline the opinions.

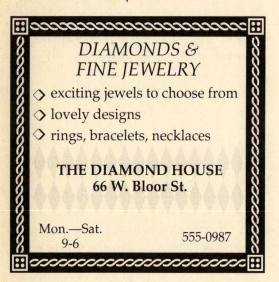

2. Underline the facts.

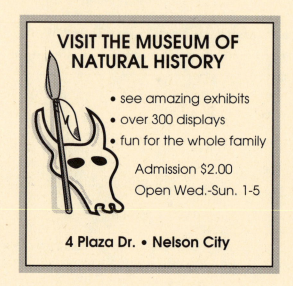

3. Underline the opinions.

4. Underline the facts.

42

STRIDES "Sarah Tops," pages 54–63
Study Skills: Advertisements

Name _____

After you read

Now write an advertisement of your own for a product or service.

▶ Include facts that your customer will need to know.
▶ Include opinions to make your customers want to buy the product or service.
▶ Illustrate your advertisement.

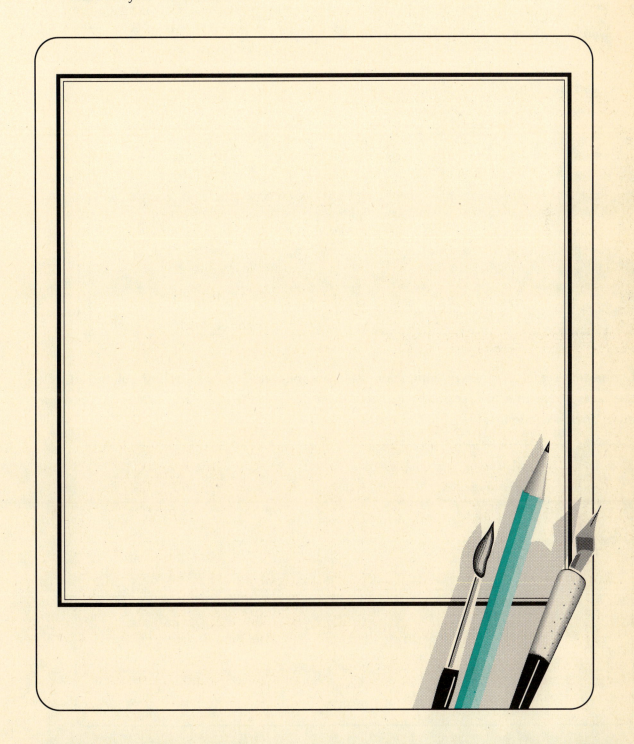

STRIDES "Sarah Tops," pages 54–63
Language: Advertisements

Name _____

An *opinion* is what someone believes, thinks, or feels about a subject. Some people may agree with the opinion. Other people may not. Read the words and phrases in the box. They are often found in statements of opinion.

| I/we believe | best/worst | I like | maybe | In my opinion |
| I/we think | smart/foolish | I feel | should | Some people say |

Now read the following list of facts:

- Scientists consider the dolphin to be the animal closest to humankind in intelligence.
- Dolphins have complicated ways of communicating with each other.
- Dolphins are social animals that help sick herd members.
- During birth, a dolphin herd will surround the mother to protect her and her newborn from predators.
- Wild dolphins have rescued people by pushing them up for air and chasing sharks away.
- Dolphins swim with humans and often let them ride on their backs.

Compose a topic sentence in which you state an opinion about protecting dolphins. Circle the facts above that best support your topic sentence. Feel free to add other facts of your own. Then write your paragraph on the lines below.

44

STRIDES "Sarah Tops," pages 54–63
Language: Supporting Opinions with Facts

Name _____

After you read

> **Remember** The *main idea* of a paragraph is the sentence that states the most important information about the topic of the paragraph.

Being able to identify the main idea of a paragraph helps the reader understand, remember, and learn from an informational article, such as "A Nation on Wheels."

Turn to "A Nation on Wheels" in *Strides,* page 64. Then follow the directions to answer each question below. Write your answers on the lines.

1. Reread paragraph 2 on page 66. Then write the sentence that states the main idea. _____
_____
_____

2. Reread paragraph 3 on page 66. Then write the sentence that states the main idea. _____
_____
_____

3. Reread paragraph 1 on page 68. Then write the sentence that states the main idea. _____
_____
_____
_____

4. Reread paragraph 2 on page 69. Then write the sentence that states the main idea. _____
_____
_____

5. Reread paragraph 1 on page 70. Then write the sentence that states the main idea. _____
_____
_____

STRIDES "A Nation on Wheels," pages 64–71
Comprehension: Stated Main Ideas of Paragraphs

After you read

Name _____

Focusing on key words can help you do well on tests. Key words such as *who*, *what*, *where*, and *when* at the beginning of questions help point to the correct answer. Use good test-taking strategies for help in choosing answers to test questions more carefully.

Here are some test questions about "A Nation on Wheels." Notice the key words in the questions. The notes at the side will help. Read each question. Fill in the circle in front of the best answer.

Key Word

1. **Who** built a steam-powered tractor to pull cannons?
   - Ⓐ France
   - Ⓑ a road vehicle
   - Ⓒ Nicolas Cugnot
   - Ⓓ three wheels

   Key word tells that the answer should be a person.

2. **Where** was car racing introduced?
   - Ⓐ rocket cars
   - Ⓑ in about 1895
   - Ⓒ 15 miles per hour
   - Ⓓ in France

   Key word tells that the answer should be a place.

3. **What** was the Stanley Steamer?
   - Ⓐ 45 minutes
   - Ⓑ Freelan and Francis Stanley
   - Ⓒ a steam-engine car
   - Ⓓ in America

   Key word tells that the answer should be a thing.

4. **When** was an early electric car built?
   - Ⓐ about 20 miles per hour
   - Ⓑ in 1890
   - Ⓒ because they were quiet
   - Ⓓ William Morrison

   Key word tells that the answer should be a time.

STRIDES "A Nation on Wheels," pages 64–71
Study Skills: Test-Taking Strategies

Name _____

Reading Guide

Using Test-Taking Strategies

When taking a test, be sure to follow this strategy:

▶ Look for key words in the questions. Words such as *who, what, where,* and *when* will help in choosing the correct answer.

Follow the directions to answer each question below.

1. Read the question.
   What did people think was a silly invention?

   a. Underline the key word in the question. Is the answer a *person, place, thing,* or *time*?

   _____

   b. Now read the question and answers. Fill in the circle in front of the best answer.
   What did people think was a silly invention?

   Ⓐ Henry Ford
   Ⓑ in 1895
   Ⓒ cars
   Ⓓ in France

2. Read the question.
   When did Ford and Oldsmobile introduce gas-powered cars?

   a. Underline the key word in the question. Is the answer a *person, place, thing,* or *time*?

   _____

   b. Now read the question and answers. Fill in the circle in front of the best answer.
   When did Ford and Oldsmobile introduce gas-powered cars?

   Ⓐ in Detroit
   Ⓑ J. Frank Duryea
   Ⓒ steam power
   Ⓓ in 1896

STRIDES "A Nation on Wheels," pages 64–71
Study Skills: Test-Taking Strategies

47

Name _____

3. Read the question.
   Who built the first successful gasoline-powered car in America?

   a. Underline the key word in the question. Is the answer a *person, place, thing,* or *time*?

   _____

   b. Now read the question and answers. Fill in the circle in front of the best answer.
      Who built the first successful gasoline-powered car in America?
      - Ⓐ an improved design
      - Ⓑ Charles and Frank Duryea
      - Ⓒ about 1895
      - Ⓓ in the United States

4. Read the question.
   Where was the Lunar Rover meant to be driven?

   a. Underline the key word in the question. Is the answer a *person, place, thing,* or *time*?

   _____

   b. Now read the question and answers. Fill in the circle in front of the best answer.
      Where was the Lunar Rover meant to be driven?
      - Ⓐ on the moon
      - Ⓑ by the U.S. Space Program
      - Ⓒ by solar power
      - Ⓓ astronauts

5. Read the question.
   What kind of car can go up to 600 miles per hour?

   a. Underline the key word in the question. Is the answer a *person, place, thing,* or *time*?

   _____

   b. Now read the question and answers. Fill in the circle in front of the best answer.
      What kind of car can go up to 600 miles per hour?
      - Ⓐ on the desert
      - Ⓑ a rocket car
      - Ⓒ in France
      - Ⓓ Henry Ford

STRIDES   "A Nation on Wheels," pages 64–71
Study Skills: Test-Taking Strategies

Name _____

Before you read

The vocabulary words below are from "An American Hero." Knowing the words and their meanings will help you understand the selection.

> academy   address   decisive   desperate
> exodus   refugees   transport   unemployment

A. Read the meaning of each word. Then follow the directions to answer the questions.

1. **refugees:** people who flee from danger.
    Which situations might cause people to become refugees? Check two.
    _____ An enemy army takes over the country.
    _____ The electricity goes off for a few hours.
    _____ The government arrests people for their beliefs.

2. **transport:** a vehicle used to carry mail, troops and military supplies, or other people or equipment.
    Which of these things would a transport do? Check two.
    _____ take troops or refugees from one place to another
    _____ carry supplies across the ocean
    _____ fish for tuna

3. **unemployment:** the state of being out of work.
    Which of these things would you expect to find during a time of high unemployment? Check two.
    _____ Everyone is working at a job.
    _____ People worry about having enough money for their needs.
    _____ People are unable to find jobs.

4. **academy:** a high school or college for advanced or specialized studies.
    Which of the following could be called an academy? Check two.
    _____ a public school
    _____ a military school
    _____ a private school that prepares students for college

5. **decisive:** important for deciding an outcome.
    Which of these might be decisive? Check two.
    _____ the color of a coat someone buys
    _____ a battle that wins a war
    _____ a point that ends a tied game

STRIDES   "An American Hero," pages 72–83
Vocabulary: Word Meanings

Before you read

Name _____

6. **desperate:** reckless because all hope or choice seems gone.
   Which of the following situations might cause a sailor to take desperate action? Check two.

   _____ Huge waves are crashing into the boat.

   _____ The boat is expected to reach the shore soon.

   _____ The boat has lost radio contact with the shore.

7. **address:** a speech.
   Which of the following could be called an address? Check two.

   _____ two friends talking together

   _____ the President speaking to Congress

   _____ a famous senator speaking to a large group of voters

8. **exodus:** a departure, or going away.
   Which of these things might cause an exodus from a town? Check two.

   _____ A hurricane is about to strike.

   _____ A new town hall is built.

   _____ There is a leak of poisonous gas.

B. **Complete each sentence. Your sentence should show that you understand the meaning of the underlined word.**

1. <u>Unemployment</u> in our town increased when _____
   _____
   _____.

2. Many <u>refugees</u> have come to the United States because _____
   _____
   _____.

3. A <u>decisive</u> moment in a person's life might be when _____
   _____
   _____.

4. The firefighter had to take <u>desperate</u> action when _____
   _____
   _____.

Name _____

A *prefix* is a word part added to the beginning of a word. The prefix changes the meaning of the word. Recognizing prefixes can help you find out the meaning of some new words.

Study the prefixes and their meanings in the box below.

PREFIX	MEANING	EXAMPLE
un-	*not* or *lack of*	unemployment
re-	*again* or *back*	repay

Notice how the prefix changes the meaning of each word:
Repay means "to pay again." *Unemployment* means "lack of employment."

Add the prefix *un-* or *re-* to the underlined word to make a new word that means the same as the words in parentheses. Write the new word on the line in the sentence.

1. Herschel was collecting _____ insurance when he came up with a great idea for a new kind of tennis shoe! (lack of employment)

2. Sitting on his porch steps watching joggers, he decided it was _____ for them to jog on hard city streets in regular tennis shoes. (not wise)

3. In college, he had helped a professor _____ a paper on how injuries to the backbone occur. (write again)

4. He was sure that running on hard pavement could _____ bones in the spine. (arrange again)

5. Herschel set out to _____ the tennis shoe. (design again)

6. Feeling it was _____ for Herschel to work without the proper equipment, the teacher loaned him money. (not fair).

7. Herschel promised to _____ his teacher within five years. (pay back).

8. Herschel had to _____ his design many times, but within three years, "City Shoes" were seen all over town. (do again)

9. Now all he had to worry about were the people who kept getting injured because they left their "City Shoes" _____! (not tied)

STRIDES   "An American Hero," pages 72–83
Vocabulary: Prefixes *un-* and *re-*

Name _____

Thinking about a selection before reading it, or *previewing* it, helps the reader to understand the selection better. One way to preview a selection is to ask questions about the title.

Below are some examples of questions a reader might ask to preview "The Pride of Madison High." Read the questions and the notes.

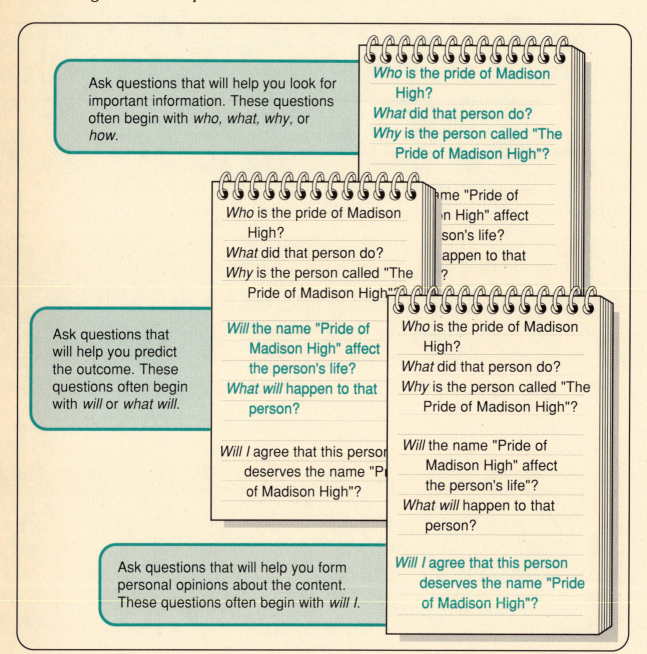

After asking questions about the title, read the selection to find the answers to these questions.

STRIDES "An American Hero," pages 72–83
Study Skills: Previewing

Name _____

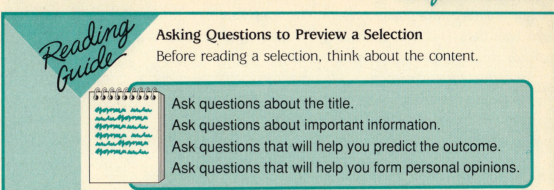

Asking Questions to Preview a Selection
Before reading a selection, think about the content.

- Ask questions about the title.
- Ask questions about important information.
- Ask questions that will help you predict the outcome.
- Ask questions that will help you form personal opinions.

A. Think about what you do before you read a selection. Read the directions and the sample responses.

Imagine that you are going to read "Sarah Tops." On the lines below, write four questions that come to your mind when you think about the title. The first word or words of each question are given.

1. Who *is Sarah Tops?*

2. Why *is Sarah Tops important to the story?*

3. What will *Sarah Tops do in the story?*

4. Will I *change my opinion of Sarah Tops as I read the story?*

STRIDES "An American Hero," pages 72–83
Study Skills: Previewing

53

Name _____

B. Imagine that you are going to read "The Four-Fifteen Express." On the lines below, write four questions that come to your mind when you think about the title. The first word or words of each question are given.

1. Who _____
_____

2. What _____
_____

3. Why _____
_____

4. What will happen _____
_____

C. The title of the next selection you will read in *Strides* is "An American Hero." On the lines below, write four questions that come to your mind when you think about the title. The first word or words of each question are given.

1. Who _____
_____

2. What _____
_____

3. Why _____
_____

4. What will _____
_____

5. Will I _____
_____

Name _____

After you read

A *conclusion* is a reasonable guess that is made by combining clues or facts with known information.

A. Below are some of Jean Nguyen's traits that can be concluded from the selection. Find one thing in the selection that Jean *says, does,* or *thinks* to show each trait.

Determined

1. _____
_____
_____

Courageous

2. _____
_____
_____

Hardworking

3. _____
_____
_____

Jean Nguyen

Strong Sense of Duty

4. _____
_____
_____

Ambitious

5. _____
_____
_____

B. Do you think that everyone in Jean's family can be called *courageous*? _____

If so, how did the family members show their courage? _____
_____

If not, why not? _____

STRIDES "An American Hero," pages 72–83
Comprehension: Conclusions—Character Traits

55

After you read

Name _____

Writers reveal a character's *traits* through the things the character does, says, and thinks. Think about how the reader found out that Jean Nguyen is hardworking. The author showed this trait through the things Jean did, such as working while going to school.

A. Read the following story opening about a working teenager. Think about the things the character does, says, and thinks. Then answer the questions.

James walked into the corner market, late as usual.

Mr. Potter eyed the clock. "I keep trying to give you a chance, son," he said sadly. Mr. Potter clicked a switch on his leg brace and sat down at a small desk behind the counter. "I was getting tired."

Shrugging his shoulders, James reached for an apron and put it on. "Boy, do I hate coming here," he thought. "Potter's always got some complaint." He paused and looked back at his boss. "I have to leave early today," he said. "I've ah . . . I've got a big test tomorrow and I've gotta study."

"I don't know, James. We've got a lot of stock to be shelved."

Just then, an elderly woman entered the shop. "Have you got any nice peaches today, young man?"

"They're all the same," said James.

"Mr. Potter always hand-selects them for me," said the woman.

James heaved a sigh and chose a few ripe peaches. He plopped them down on the counter.

1. What does James *do* that shows irresponsibility? _____
   _____

2. What does James *think* that indicates he is self-centered? _____
   _____
   _____

3. What does James *say* that shows he doesn't take his responsibilities seriously? _____
   _____
   _____

4. What does James *say* that is rude? _____
   _____

5. What does James *do* in an uncooperative way? _____
   _____

STRIDES "An American Hero," pages 72–83
Language: Character Traits in Writing

Name _____

After you read

B. Rewrite the story opening about James and Mr. Potter so that James is responsible, polite, and helpful. Leave the characters in the same setting, but change what James does, says, and thinks so that these new character traits are revealed.

STRIDES "An American Hero," pages 72–83
Language: Character Traits in Writing

Name _____

The vocabulary words below are from "A Change for the Better." Knowing the words and their meanings will help you understand the selection.

> concentrating dreading exhausted hammock
> impatiently omelet remarriage

Context clues are the other words and phrases that help you understand an unfamiliar word in a sentence or a paragraph.

A. Read each sentence. Use the context clues to help you find out the meaning of the underlined word. Circle the letter in front of the best answer. Then underline the context clues that helped you.

1. The runners were exhausted after running five miles. In the sentence, *exhausted* means _____.

   a. gas from a car **b.** very tired **c.** ready to begin

2. Jessie was concentrating so hard on a book that she didn't even hear the phone ring. In the sentence, *concentrating* means _____.

   a. thinking hard **b.** listening **c.** daydreaming

3. Because of my mother's remarriage, I now have a stepfather. In the sentence, *remarriage* means _____.

   a. the condition of being married again **b.** being born **c.** going away

4. The cook used eggs, tomatoes, and onions to make an omelet for breakfast. In the sentence, *omelet* means _____.

   a. kitchen **b.** a dish made of eggs **c.** a type of pan

5. The crowd waited impatiently as eight o'clock passed, and the play still hadn't begun. In the sentence, *impatiently* means _____.

   a. slowly **b.** not sick **c.** without patience

6. A hammock stretched between two trees is a good place for a nap. In the sentence, *hammock* means _____.

   a. a type of hanging bed **b.** mushroom **c.** large basket

7. Although she is usually not afraid of tests, Tanya is dreading her science test since she didn't study. In the sentence, *dreading* means _____.

   a. hoping **b.** thinking about with fear **c.** trying hard

58 STRIDES "A Change for the Better," pages 86–101
Vocabulary: Context Clues

Name _____

B. Complete each sentence below. Your sentence should show that you understand the meaning of the underlined word.

1. If I were making an <u>omelet</u>, I would _____
   _____
   _____ .

2. Nothing makes a person more <u>exhausted</u> than _____
   _____
   _____ .

3. I always wait <u>impatiently</u> when I am waiting for _____
   _____
   _____ .

4. Right now some people are probably <u>dreading</u> _____
   _____
   _____ .

5. It would be nice to place a <u>hammock</u> _____
   _____
   _____ .

6. Because of a parent's <u>remarriage</u>, a son or daughter might have to _____
   _____
   _____ .

7. <u>Concentrating</u> on good music _____
   _____ .

STRIDES "A Change for the Better," pages 86–101
Vocabulary: Context Clues

Name _____

When you tell someone what happened in a story, you are telling the story *plot*. The plot of a story has a structure, or shape.

Study the map below. It shows the four parts of a story plot.

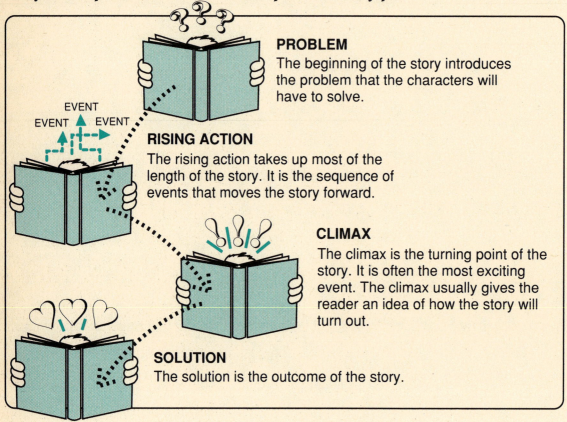

PROBLEM
The beginning of the story introduces the problem that the characters will have to solve.

RISING ACTION
The rising action takes up most of the length of the story. It is the sequence of events that moves the story forward.

CLIMAX
The climax is the turning point of the story. It is often the most exciting event. The climax usually gives the reader an idea of how the story will turn out.

SOLUTION
The solution is the outcome of the story.

The example shows the parts of the plot of a familiar fairy tale.

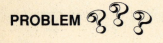 Snow White's life is in danger because she is considered lovelier than her stepmother, the queen.

• A servant takes Snow White deep into the forest and tells her to hide from the queen, who wants her dead.
• The queen finds out that Snow White is still alive and disguises herself as an old woman and goes to the seven dwarfs' house.
• Snow White takes a bite of a poison apple given to her by the old woman and falls into a deep sleep.

 A prince finds Snow White and awakens her with a kiss.

 The prince and Snow White marry and live happily ever after.

STRIDES   "A Change for the Better," pages 86–101
Comprehension: Plot

Name _____

Reading Guide

Identifying Plot

As you read, look for the main parts of the plot:

- problem (introduction)
- rising action (events)
- climax (turning point)
- solution (outcome)

A. As you read each story, look for the main parts of the plot. Then read the questions and the answers.

Five-year-old J.T. could hardly talk through his tears. "I lost my kite!" he sobbed. "It was way up in the air, and the string broke. Now I'll never see it again!"

His brother Tony wished he could promise J.T. a new kite, but he knew there was no money for one. What could he do to make J.T. feel better? Tony was still thinking about the problem later that evening as he took out the garbage.

"Maybe I could make a kite," he thought. "But I don't have any cloth. I wonder—" His eye fell on the black plastic garbage bag he was carrying. "That's it!" he cried.

The next day J.T. was proudly flying a new kite made from the heavy plastic bag and some thin strips of cardboard cut from a milk carton. It looked just like a huge black bat!

1. What is the *problem*? _J.T. has lost his kite._

2. What is the *climax* of the story? _Tony notices the plastic garbage bag and realizes he can make a kite from it._
   How do you know? _It is the turning point in the story._

3. What is the *solution* to the problem in the story? _Tony makes J.T. a new kite from the garbage bag and a milk carton._

STRIDES "A Change for the Better," pages 86–101
Comprehension: Plot

61

Name _____

B. Read the story. Then read the questions and write your answers on the lines.

Pat sat on his bed and thought about how unhappy he was. He had been upset about moving since his parents had made the decision. Now they had been living in Kentfield for three weeks. Pat hated it. He had no friends.

Pat's thoughts were interrupted by the telephone. It was Mark, a boy in his math class. "Want to go with Ken and me to the football game tonight?" he asked.

"No, I can't. I have to do some things at home," Pat told Mark. As quickly as he could, he hung up.

Just then Mark's mother entered the room. "I heard your telephone conversation," she said. "I don't understand. You're unhappy about having no friends, but you don't try to make any. Mark has called three times to invite you somewhere. Two other boys have called, too. You always say no. How do you expect to make friends if you don't try? It's a two-way street. You have to make an effort to be a friend before you can have a friend."

Pat said nothing. His mother walked out of the room. He sat and thought about what she had said. "Maybe she's right," he thought. "I've been so unhappy about moving that I haven't made an effort to be a friend."

A few minutes later, Pat picked up the phone and dialed Mark's number. When Mark answered, Pat said, "Is that invitation to the game still open? I'd really like to go with you."

1. What is the *problem*? _____
_____
_____

2. What is the *climax* of the story? _____
_____
_____

How do you know? _____
_____
_____

3. What is the *solution* to the problem in the story? _____
_____
_____

Name _____

C. **Think about the strategies you used to answer the questions in part B. Then read the story and answer the questions.**

   Usually Teresa loved to visit the Museum of Natural History. Today, though, she had to bring her little stepbrother, Miguel. Ever since her father had remarried, it had been that way. She had to take Miguel everywhere she went. As usual he was a pest, whining about how tired he was. Teresa tried to ignore Miguel as she stood and stared at the huge skeleton of a dinosaur. She tried to imagine what it must have been like to live when these gigantic creatures roamed the earth. Then she turned to take Miguel's hand to go on to the next display, but he wasn't there! She looked around and called his name. He was gone!

   As Teresa searched the entire room, she began to think of all the horrible things that could have happened to Miguel. She felt a wave of fear wash over her. Even though he could be a bother, she did love Miguel. She hurried down to the front desk near the museum entrance to report that Miguel was missing. Teresa told her story, and three security guards began searching.

   As Teresa was looking under the case displaying arrowheads, she recalled Miguel's fascination with the American Indian homes. She also remembered how he had complained of being tired. She ran to the third floor, into the room with the tepees and lodges.

   Teresa climbed up onto the display platform and looked into the first tepee. There was Miguel, curled up on a blanket, sound asleep. Teresa signaled to a guard that she had found Miguel.

   When Teresa woke Miguel, he smiled and crawled into her arms. She was about to scold him, but she gave him a big hug instead.

1. What is the *problem*? _____

_____

2. What is the *climax* of the story? _____

_____

_____

How do you know? _____

_____

3. What is the *solution* to the problem in the story? _____

_____

STRIDES "A Change for the Better," pages 86–101
Comprehension: Plot

63

After you read

Name _____

Remember The *plot* is the action of the story. The plot of a story has a structure, or shape. It has four parts arranged in a certain way.

Use the story map on study guide page 60 and the selection to answer questions about the parts of the plot of "A Change for the Better." Circle the letter in front of the best answer, or write the answers on the lines.

1. In the first part of the story, the author presents the *problem*. What is it?
   a. Beth doesn't like Susan and Linda.
   b. Beth is unhappy because she cannot accept the changes in her life.
   c. Beth goes to the movies instead of eating dinner with her family.

2. Below are two events in the *rising action* of the story. List three more events that are part of the rising action.
   a. Beth uses Linda's bicycle without permission.
   b. Beth leaves Linda's bicycle unlocked while she goes to the movies.

   c. _____

   d. _____

   e. _____

3. What is the *climax* of the story? At what point in the story do you first realize how it will end?
   a. when Beth talks with Susan and discovers that Linda, too, is having trouble adjusting to changes in her life
   b. when Beth cooks breakfast with Linda
   c. when Linda goes to the police station to get her bicycle

4. What is the *solution* to the story problem?
   a. Beth decides not to fight the changes in her life and begins to take steps to get along with her new family.
   b. Linda gets her bicycle back.
   c. Beth thinks about what her father said about not taking others' property.

Name _____

Every library has a card catalog to help readers find the books they want. The *card catalog* is a set of cards in drawers. Each card lists a book in the library, describes it, and tells where the book can be found. The library has three kinds of cards for each book.

SUBJECT CARD

The subject card gives the subject heading, or topic, first. Use a subject card if you want to find a book on a certain topic but do not know or remember the title or author of a particular book.

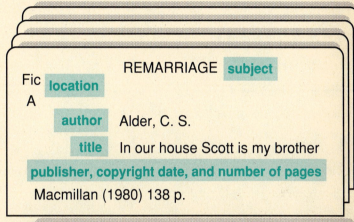

AUTHOR CARD

On an author card, the author's name is on the top line. Use this card if you are looking for a book by a particular author.

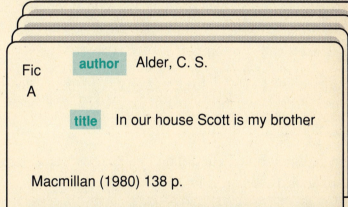

TITLE CARD

On a title card, the book's title is on the top line. Use this card if you know the title of the book you want.

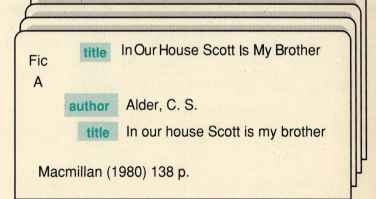

STRIDES "A Change for the Better," pages 86–101
Study Skills: Library—Card Catalog

Name _____

Use the information about how a card catalog is organized to help you answer each question below. Circle the letter in front of the correct answer.

1. Beth wants to read a book about stepsisters. She has no special book in mind. What type of card should she use to find a book on that topic?

   a. subject   **b.** author   **c.** title

2. Linda wants to check out a book that Beth recommended. It's called *Twink*. What type of card should she use to find it?

   a. subject   **b.** author   **c.** title

3. Beth just finished a book by Nina Bawden and really liked it. She wants to read another book by the same author. What type of card should she use to find it?

   a. subject   **b.** author   **c.** title

4. Linda wants to read *Footsteps on the Stairs*. What type of card should she use to find it?

   a. subject   **b.** author   **c.** title

5. Beth wants to try to get along better with Susan. She decides to read some books about stepfamilies. What type of card should she use to find a book on that topic?

   a. subject   **b.** author   **c.** title

6. Susan wants to find out if the library has any books about how to help family members get along. She knows she should use a subject card. Under what heading should she look?

   a. family relationships   **b.** children   **c.** friends

7. Linda wants to find out if John Neufield has written any books besides *Twink*. What type of card should she use to find a book by that author?

   a. subject   **b.** author   **c.** title

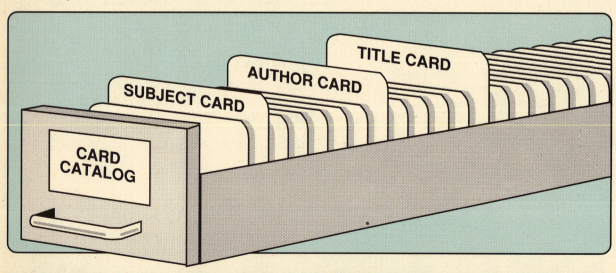

Name _____

Every story has a plot. The plot is built around a conflict, or struggle. There are two kinds of conflicts: *internal* and *external*.

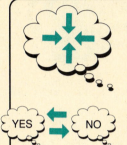

An internal conflict is a struggle within a character's mind. For example, in "The Race to Dog Tail Island," Carmen is trying to overcome her fear of swimming.

An external conflict is a struggle between forces. It can be between or among persons. In "Sarah Tops," Larry and his detective dad struggle to find a stolen diamond. An external conflict can also be between a person and nature.

Read each question. Think about the plot of "A Change for the Better." Circle the letter in front of the correct answer, or write the answer on the lines.

1. The main conflict in the story is an *internal* one. What is the *internal* conflict in the story?
    a. Linda's struggle to change her feelings toward Beth
    b. Beth's struggle to accept the changes in her life
    c. Susan's struggle to win Beth's friendship

2. Before the story begins, what event happened that set up an *internal* conflict? _____
   _____

3. How does the description of Beth's room show the *internal* conflict in the story? _____
   _____
   _____
   _____
   _____

4. What is the *external* conflict in the story?
    a. Beth's struggle to get along with Susan
    b. Beth's struggle to find Linda's bicycle
    c. Beth's struggle to accept change

5. Which events in the story are proof of an external conflict? Choose two.
    a. Beth's criticism of Susan's cooking
    b. Beth's talking to her father about losing Linda's bicycle
    c. Beth's ignoring Susan's question and answering the telephone
    d. Beth's hugging her father

STRIDES   "A Change for the Better," pages 86–101
Literature: Conflict

Name _____

The vocabulary words below are from "Volcano!" Knowing the words and their meanings will help you understand the selection.

> absolute   eruption   geologist
> suffocating   volcano

Context clues are the other words and phrases that help you understand an unfamiliar word in a sentence or a paragraph.

Read each paragraph. Use the context clues to help you decide what the underlined word means. Circle the letter in front of the correct answer. Underline the words and phrases that helped you find out the meaning.

1. The volcano burst apart with a deafening roar. It took only a few minutes for melted rock and burning cinders to bury everything on the mountainside.
   In the paragraph, *volcano* means _____.
   a. a steep slope of a mountain
   b. an opening in the earth's surface
   c. a container for coal

2. The eruption of a volcano is a terrifying event. Tons of rock blow high into the sky. A swirling black cloud hides the sun.
   In the paragraph, *eruption* means _____.
   a. a violent explosion of rock   b. a quiet time after an explosion   c. a bad storm

3. A geologist studies the way the earth is formed. He or she also studies the history of rocks and the soil.
   In the paragraph, *geologist* means _____.
   a. a person who lives in Germany
   b. a person who is quiet and gentle
   c. a person who studies the structure of the earth

4. The suffocating heat in the tiny room made my chest feel as if it were about to burst. My lungs begged for air.
   In the paragraph, *suffocating* means _____.
   a. covering with a heavy cloth
   b. causing difficulty in breathing
   c. causing a burn

5. There was absolute quiet when the principal spoke. No one made any noise at all.
   In the paragraph, *absolute* means _____.
   a. complete   b. courteous   c. nearly

Name _____

Many words in English have *multiple meanings,* or more than one meaning. These words can be understood only when they appear in sentences. Context clues can help the reader decide which meaning the writer has in mind.

The words below are from "Volcano!" Both of them have multiple meanings.

Shock means
1. a strong, sudden jolt or shake
2. a weakening of the body because of injury
3. a jolt from an electric current
4. a sudden and severe upset of the mind or feelings

Ash means
1. a shade tree
2. a fine, white powder left after something has burned

Read each question. Write your answers on the lines.

1. Read each sentence. Then write the meaning of *shock* as it is used in the sentence.
   a. I'll never forget the *shock* of hearing that the house was destroyed by the explosion.

   In this sentence, *shock* means _____

   _____.

   b. Doctors watched Alan for signs of *shock* after the explosion knocked him to the ground.

   In this sentence, *shock* means _____

   _____.

2. Write a sentence using *shock*. In your sentence, *shock* should mean "a jolt from an electric current." _____

   _____

3. Write a sentence using *ash*. In your sentence, *ash* should mean "a fine, white powder left after something has burned."

   _____

   _____

4. Write a sentence using *ash*. In your sentence, *ash* should mean "a shade tree."

   _____

   _____

STRIDES "Volcano!" pages 116–129
Vocabulary: Multiple Meanings

Name _____

Cause-and-effect relationships show how one event leads to another.

Study the cause-and-effect map below.

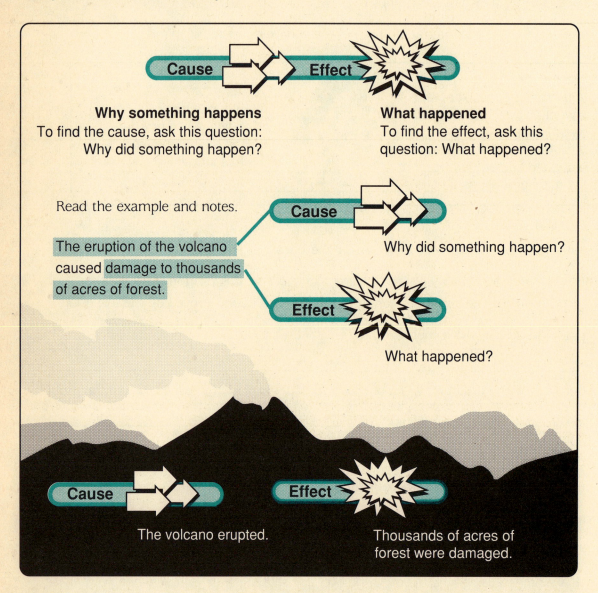

Sometimes a writer signals a cause-and-effect relationship with certain words and phrases.

In the example above, *caused* is the word that signals a cause-and-effect relationship.

CAUSE-AND-EFFECT SIGNAL WORDS		
because	therefore	since
then	caused	due to
resulted in	as a result of	

STRIDES "Volcano!" pages 116–129
Comprehension: Causes and Effects

Name _____

Reading Guide

Identifying Causes and Effects

As you read, be sure to ask yourself these questions:

▶ *Why did something happen?*
   The answer to the question is the *cause*.
▶ *What happened?*
   The answer to the question is the *effect*.
▶ Are there cause-and-effect signal words?
   Remember that a writer does not always use them.

Cause ➡ Effect

A. As you read each sentence, think about the cause and the effect. Read the questions and the answers.

1. The eruption of the volcano resulted in hundreds of deaths.

   a. *Effect:* What happened when the volcano erupted? _Hundreds of people died._

   b. Is there a word or a phrase that signals a cause-and-effect relationship? ___yes___ If yes, what is it? ___resulted in___

2. Snow on the mountain melted as a result of the heat from the eruption.

   a. The snow melted. *Cause:* Why did this happen? _It happened because of the heat from the eruption._

   b. Is there a word or a phrase that signals a cause-and-effect relationship? ___yes___ If yes, what is it? ___as a result of___

STRIDES "Volcano!" pages 116–129
Comprehension: Causes and Effects

Name _____

B. Read each sentence. Then read the questions and write your answers on the lines.

1. The eruption of one volcano was so powerful that it caused a change in the climate.

   a. The climate changed. *Cause:* Why did this happen? _____
   _____

   b. Is there a word or a phrase that signals a cause-and-effect relationship?
   _____ If yes, what is it? _____

2. Huge mudslides destroyed houses, roads, and bridges.

   a. *Effect:* What happened when there were mudslides? _____
   _____

   b. Is there a word or a phrase that signals a cause-and-effect relationship?
   _____ If yes, what is it? _____

C. Think about the strategies you used to answer the questions in part B. Then answer the questions and fill in the map.

1. Dangerous fires and floods threatened the countryside as a result of the eruption.

   Effect: What happened because of the eruption? _____
   _____

2. Volcanic ash and dust spread over the countryside. The next year, farmers found that their land was more fertile.

   The land became more fertile. *Cause:* Why did this happen? _____
   _____

3. A great mudflow jammed thousands of logs in the stream, and the bridge collapsed.

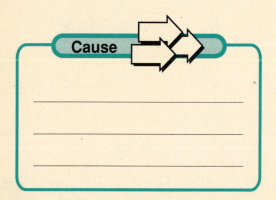

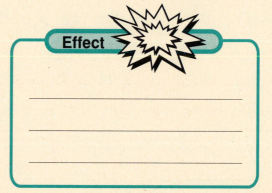

STRIDES "Volcano!" pages 116–129
Comprehension: Causes and Effects

Name _____

 The *cause* is the reason something happens. It comes first in time. An *effect* always happens as a result of a cause.

Follow the directions to answer the questions. Write the answers on the lines in complete sentences. Use the selection "Volcano!" for help.

1. Find the *cause*. Why had burning ash and mud smothered absolutely everything on all sides of the mountain? (page 117, paragraph 1)

   _____
   _____

2. Find the *effect*. What happened when the black cloud of ash began to rise? (page 122, paragraph 3)

   _____
   _____

3. Find the *effect*. What happened to Karen and Terry? (page 126, paragraph 1)

   _____
   _____

4. Find the *effect*. What happened to Brian? (page 126, paragraph 6)

   _____
   _____

5. Find the *cause*. Why were the people in the helicopter able to spot Bruce and Sue? (page 128, paragraph 1)

   _____
   _____

6. Find the *effect*. What happened to Harry Truman? (page 128, paragraph 2)

   _____
   _____

STRIDES "Volcano!" pages 116–129
Comprehension: Causes and Effects

Name _____

An *index* is an alphabetical listing of the names, places, and subjects that can be found in a book, along with their page numbers. Indexes are found at the back of many books. Information is grouped according to *topics* and *subtopics*. By using the index, a reader can locate information in a book quickly and easily.

Below is a section of an index from a book. Use the notes to study this section of the index.

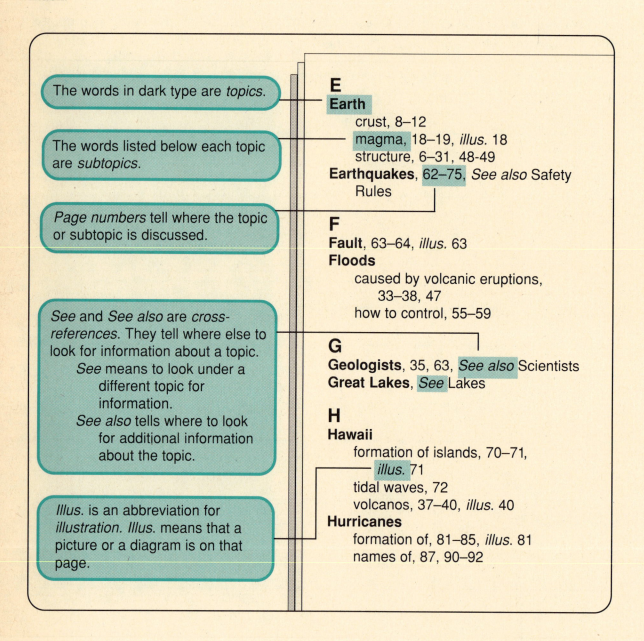

STRIDES "Volcano!" pages 116–129
Study Skills: Parts of a Book—Index

Name _____

After you read

Use the sample index on page 74 to answer the questions below. Circle the letter in front of the correct answer.

1. The topics in the index are listed _____.
   a. by subject   b. alphabetically   c. by page number

2. The words in dark type are _____.
   a. illustrations   b. subtopics   c. topics

3. On which pages would you find information on how to control floods?
   a. 33, 38, 47   b. 56, 57, 58   c. 38, 47, 59

4. How many subtopics are under the topic *Hurricanes*?
   a. two   b. three   c. none

5. If you wanted to find out some safety rules to follow in an earthquake, under what heading would you look for additional information?
   a. Floods   b. Safety Rules   c. Survival

6. Which word or words tell you that you will find the information you need under a different topic?
   a. See also   b. See   c. illus.

7. If you wanted to find out how hurricanes are formed, under what topic would you look?
   a. Names   b. Hurricanes   c. Formation

8. Which page has an illustration of a fault?
   a. 60   b. 64   c. 63

9. Under what topic should you look to find information about the Great Lakes?
   a. Michigan   b. Bodies of Water   c. Lakes

STRIDES "Volcano!" pages 116–129
Study Skills: Parts of a Book—Index

Name _____

Writers use *descriptive words and phrases* to help the reader form a mental picture of where a story takes place.

Use the information in "Volcano!" and your imagination to describe where the selection takes place. List as many details as you can.

1. Imagine that you are Sue or Bruce. It is early Sunday morning, May 18, 1980. Mount St. Helens has not yet erupted. Think about what you see, hear, smell, and feel on the peaceful mountain. Then fill in the chart with descriptive words and phrases.

	See	
	Hear	
	Smell	
	Feel	

2. Now imagine that Mount St. Helens has just erupted. Think about what you see, hear, smell, and feel. Then fill in the chart with descriptive words and phrases.

	See	
	Hear	
	Smell	
	Feel	

Name _____

After you read

Read "Dust Storm!" below. Imagine that you are there when the dust storm occurs. Think about what you see, hear, smell, and feel. Then fill in the chart with descriptive words and phrases.

Dust Storm!

It was my first trip to Carefree, Arizona. I was relaxing on a raft in my cousin Natalie's pool. Suddenly, Natalie flew out of the house. "Dust storm!" she shouted. "Help me close the windows!"

She was pointing over the backyard wall. I looked. The nearby mountains had disappeared. A heavy darkness filled the sky. I jumped out of the pool and dried off. The sharp clang of metal filled my ears as Natalie folded the lawn chairs and stacked them in a corner of the patio.

We rushed into the house and ran from room to room sliding windows down and locking them in place. As I closed a bedroom window, I could see the darkness nearing the house. Then, smack! I felt the wind slap the house. As it struggled to get inside, I could smell the stale odor of dust.

When the wind stopped, we walked back outside. Everywhere, everything was covered with a gritty, brown layer of dust. "Carefree?" I said, laughing. "You almost had me fooled!"

See	
Hear	
Smell	
Feel	

STRIDES "Volcano!" pages 116–129
Language: Descriptive Language

Name _____

The main idea of a paragraph is the sentence that tells the most important idea about the topic. It may be the first sentence in the paragraph, or it may be another sentence.

Supporting details are all the other sentences in the paragraph that tell about the main idea.

Use the selection "What Will They Think of Next?" to answer the questions below. Write the answers on the lines.

1. a. Which sentence states the main idea of the paragraph "Cans That Chill"? _____
   _____
   _____

   b. Where in the paragraph is the main idea sentence? _____
   _____

2. a. Which sentence states the main idea of the paragraph "Bath Machine"? _____
   _____
   _____

   b. Where in the paragraph is the main idea sentence? _____
   _____

3. a. Which sentence states the main idea of the paragraph "New Clothes"? _____
   _____
   _____

   b. Where in the paragraph is the main idea sentence? _____
   _____

4. a. Which sentence states the main idea of the last paragraph of the selection? _____
   _____
   _____

   b. Where in the paragraph is the main idea sentence? _____
   _____

STRIDES "What Will They Think of Next?" pages 130–133
Comprehension: Stated Main Ideas of Paragraphs

Name _____

After you read

Below is a test question for "What Will They Think of Next?" Read the question and all of the answers. Notice how well the key word in the question goes with the answer choices. The notes at the side will help you.

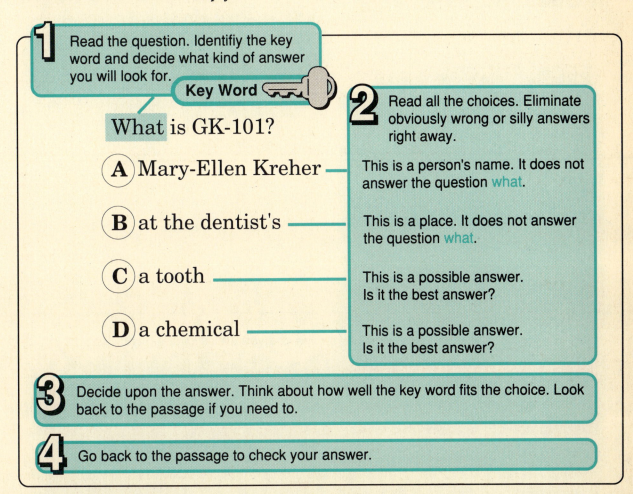

1 Read the question. Identify the key word and decide what kind of answer you will look for.

Key Word

What is GK-101?

A Mary-Ellen Kreher — This is a person's name. It does not answer the question *what*.

B at the dentist's — This is a place. It does not answer the question *what*.

C a tooth — This is a possible answer. Is it the best answer?

D a chemical — This is a possible answer. Is it the best answer?

2 Read all the choices. Eliminate obviously wrong or silly answers right away.

3 Decide upon the answer. Think about how well the key word fits the choice. Look back to the passage if you need to.

4 Go back to the passage to check your answer.

Reading Guide

Using Test-Taking Strategies

When answering test questions, follow these steps:

▶ Read the question. Identify the key word and decide what type of answer you are looking for.

▶ Read all the choices. Eliminate obviously wrong or silly answers right away.

▶ Decide upon the answer. Think about how well the key word in the question goes with each choice. Look back to the passage if necessary.

▶ ALWAYS go back to the passage to check your answer.

STRIDES   "What Will They Think of Next?" pages 130–133
Study Skills: Test-Taking Strategies

After you read

Name _____

Follow the directions to answer each question below.

A. Read the question.
   Through what does a tubecraft run?

1. What key word in the question tells you the type of answer to look for?

   _____

2. Circle the letter in front of the type of answer you are looking for.
   a. person   b. object or event   c. place   d. time words

3. Now read the question and all the answer choices.
   Through what does a tubecraft run?
   Ⓐ New York   Ⓒ a tunnel
   Ⓑ inventor   Ⓓ in the future

   Which answer choices can you eliminate right away? _____
   _____

   Why? _____

4. Fill in the circle in front of the best answer. How did you choose the answer? _____
   _____

B. Read the question.
   Where is GK-101 sprayed?

1. What key word in the question tells you the type of answer to look for?

   _____

2. Circle the letter in front of the type of answer you are looking for.
   a. person   b. object or event   c. place   d. time words

3. Now read the question and all the answer choices.
   Where is GK-101 sprayed?
   Ⓐ on a decayed tooth   Ⓒ in a few minutes
   Ⓑ next year   Ⓓ a type of drill

   Which answer choices can you eliminate right away? _____
   _____

   Why? _____

STRIDES "What Will They Think of Next?" pages 130–133
Study Skills: Test-Taking Strategies

Name _____

4. Fill in the circle in front of the best answer. How did you choose the answer? _____
_____
_____

C. Read the question.

   When does the freezing unit of a Chill Can begin to work?

1. What key word in the question tells you the type of answer to look for?
   _____

2. Circle the letter in front of the type of answer you are looking for.
   a. person   c. place
   b. object or event d. time words

3. Now read the question and all the answer choices.

   When does the freezing unit of a Chill Can begin to work?
   Ⓐ inside the can   Ⓒ wherever it is taken
   Ⓑ a cold drink   Ⓓ as soon as the can is opened

   Which answer choices can you eliminate right away? _____
   _____

   Why? _____
   _____
   _____

4. Fill in the circle in front of the best answer. How did you choose the answer? _____
_____
_____

STRIDES "What Will They Think of Next?" pages 130–133
Study Skills: Test-Taking Strategies

Before you read

Name _____

In a dictionary or a glossary, *guide words* are at the top of each page. The guide word on the left tells the first word on the page. The guide word on the right tells the last word on the page. Using the guide words will help you find a word in a dictionary or a glossary more quickly.

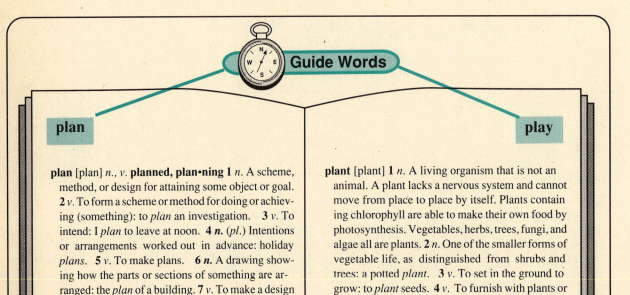

The two words in dark print at the top of each list are the guide words on a dictionary page. Read each question. If the underlined word would be on the *same* dictionary page as the guide words, circle A. If the underlined word would be on a page *before* the page with the guide words, circle B. If the underlined word would be on a page *after* the page with the guide words, circle C.

elevator – elm

1. Where would you find ele<u>phant</u>?
   A same page   B before   C after

2. Where would you find e<u>lf</u>?
   A same page   B before   C after

3. Where would you find e<u>lse</u>?
   A same page   B before   C after

4. Where would you find e<u>lect</u>?
   A same page   B before   C after

dream – drizzle

5. Where would you find d<u>redge</u>?
   A same page   B before   C after

6. Where would you find d<u>riveway</u>?
   A same page   B before   C after

7. Where would you find d<u>raw</u>?
   A same page   B before   C after

8. Where would you find d<u>rop</u>?
   A same page   B before   C after

STRIDES "Twenty-Two," pages 134–145
Study Skills: Dictionary—Guide Words and Entry

Name _____

Before you read

A dictionary entry gives the meanings of words and information about how to say, spell, and use the words.

Below is an entry from a dictionary. The notes tell what each part of the entry means.

> The *entry word* is in dark type. Dots show where the word is divided into syllables.
>
> The pronunciation of each word (the way it is said) is spelled in a special way. The letters that stand for the sounds are explained in the pronunciation key, which is usually found at the bottom of each right-hand page.
>
> The abbreviation for the *part of speech* of the word is in *italics*.
>
> The *definition* gives the word's meaning.
>
> **prog•no•sis** (prog•nō´sis) *n.* A prediction about the future course of a disease and the patient's chances of recovery.

Use the information above and a dictionary to answer the questions. Write the answers on the lines.

1. What does the special spelling of *prognosis* tell you? _____
_____
_____

2. What does *prognosis* mean? _____
_____
_____

3. In a dictionary, look up *fatigued*. What guide words are on the same page? _____
_____

4. What is the entry word for *fatigued*? _____

5. What is the meaning of *fatiguing*? _____
_____

STRIDES "Twenty-Two," pages 134–145
Study Skills: Dictionary—Guide Words and Entry

Name _____

The vocabulary words below are from "Twenty-Two." Knowing the words and their meanings will help you understand the selection.

> acute   anxiety   diagnosis
> fatigue morgue   narrator

Context clues are the other words and phrases that help you understand an unfamiliar word in a sentence or a paragraph.

Read each sentence. Use the context clues to help you find out the meaning of the underlined word. Circle the letter in front of the correct answer. Underline the words and phrases that help you find out the meaning.

1. The unidentified body will be held in the morgue until it is examined to find out how the man died. In the sentence, *morgue* means _____.
   a. the emergency room of a hospital
   b. a special table for moving sick people in a hospital
   c. a place where dead bodies are kept for examination

2. The illness that started so suddenly and turned out to be so serious was acute food poisoning. In the sentence, *acute* means _____.
   a. very mild   b. very serious   c. very delicious

3. After Dr. Wilson had carefully examined my ears, he told me that his diagnosis was an ear infection. In the sentence, *diagnosis* means _____.
   a. a medical explanation for an illness
   b. an estimate of the time needed to recover from an illness
   c. a picture or a graph used in medical testing

4. Many people who fly in airplanes suffer from anxiety because they are so uneasy about what they think may happen. In the sentence, *anxiety* means _____.
   a. a calm feeling   b. a happy feeling   c. a worried feeling

5. The mountain climbers were treated at the hospital for fatigue after their long, exhausting hike. In the sentence, *fatigue* means _____.
   a. an infection   b. a tired condition   c. hunger

6. The narrator introduced the play and told about scenes that were not included in the presentation. In the sentence, *narrator* means _____.
   a. the director of a play   b. the play's author
   c. someone who explains a presentation or comments on it

STRIDES "Twenty-Two," pages 134–145
Vocabulary: Context Clues

Name _____

Before you read

An *antonym* is a word that means the opposite of another word. Writers may use antonyms to show how two things are different.

A. The words below are from the selection "Twenty-Two." Find each word in the dictionary. Then write its meaning on the line.

1. discharge: _____

2. departing: _____

3. fatigue: _____

4. phantom: _____

5. rejecting: _____

B. The words in the box are antonyms of the words above. Use the words in the box to fill in the chart.

| imprison   real   accepting   energy   arriving |

WORD	ANTONYM
1. discharge	
2. departing	
3. fatigue	
4. phantom	
5. rejecting	

C. Look at the pairs of antonyms above. Choose two pairs. Use each word in a sentence of your own.

1. _____

_____

2. _____

_____

STRIDES "Twenty-Two," pages 134–145
Vocabulary: Antonyms

Name _____

A *comparison* tells how two or more people, places, or items are alike. A *contrast* tells how two or more people, places, or items are different.

Read the passage to compare and contrast these types of nightmares.

   A nightmare is a frightening dream. Normal nightmares occur during regular sleep and awaken the sleeper. Once awake, the sleeper can remember the dream that scared him or her.

   A night terror attack is a special type of nightmare. It occurs when people are in deep sleep. People who experience night terrors report that they feel a pressure on their chests, as if a heavy weight were resting on them. They wake up terrified. In most cases they don't remember the nightmare at all.

The diagram below shows how information about each type of nightmare has been organized separately.

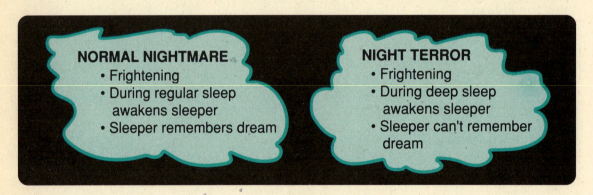

The diagram below shows how to compare and contrast the two types of nightmares. It shows how the types of nightmares are alike and different.

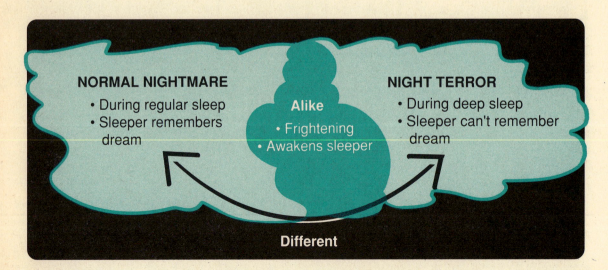

Name _____

Reading Guide

Making Comparisons and Contrasts
Follow these steps to make comparisons and contrasts from several paragraphs in a selection:

- First, organize the information about each person, place, or item to be compared and contrasted.
- Next, compare and contrast the information. Ask:
  How are these alike?
  How are these different?   different alike different

A. As you read the passage, think about how the information should be organized. Read the questions and the answers.

   My brother Edward is one of those people who need at least eight hours of sleep each night. He goes to sleep easily and sleeps through the night without waking up. He says that he usually has several pleasant dreams each night.
   My sister Peggy also needs eight hours of sleep. She goes to sleep right away, but she wakes up two or three times during the night. She says she dreams quite a bit but often has nightmares.

1. Organize the information about each person's sleeping habits.

Edward	Peggy
needs eight hours of sleep	needs eight hours of sleep
goes to sleep easily	goes to sleep easily
sleeps without waking up	wakes up during the night
has pleasant dreams	often has nightmares

2. Now compare the information. List two ways that their sleeping habits are alike.

   a. *They both need eight hours of sleep.*

   b. *They both go to sleep easily.*

3. Now contrast the information. List two ways that their sleeping habits are different.

   a. *One sleeps without waking up; the other wakes up during the night.*

   b. *One has pleasant dreams; the other often has nightmares.*

STRIDES "Twenty-Two," pages 134–145
Comprehension: Comparisons and Contrasts

Name _____

B. Read the passage. Then read the questions and write your answers on the lines.

Both my brother and my father sleepwalk. When Miguel sleepwalks, he sits or stands near his bed. He never goes anywhere. He says that he never remembers getting up and that it usually happens when he is worried about school. The next day, he wakes up feeling well rested.

When my father sleepwalks, he wanders around the house. We're afraid he'll fall on the stairs or trip over something. Dad never remembers walking around in his sleep, nor does he know why he sleepwalks. But it seems to me that it happens when he is worried about things at work. Even though he sleepwalks, Dad wakes up rested.

1. Organize the information about each person's sleepwalking.

   Miguel   **Dad**

   _____   _____
   _____   _____
   _____   _____
   _____   _____

2. Now compare the information. List three ways that their sleepwalking is alike.

   a. _____
      _____

   b. _____
      _____

   c. _____
      _____

3. Now contrast the information. Write one way that their sleepwalking is different.

   _____
   _____
   _____

STRIDES "Twenty-Two," pages 134–145
Comprehension: Comparisons and Contrasts

Name _____

Before you read

C. Think about the strategies you used to answer the questions in part B. Then answer the questions.

    There are two dreams that I keep having over and over. In one I am on my way to the airport to catch a plane. We leave on time, but we get stuck in terrible traffic. We sit and sit on the freeway. As the time ticks away, I become more and more anxious. Finally, the cars begin to move. We get to the airport a few minutes before the plane is scheduled to take off. I run through the airport toward the gate. I keep running and running, but I can't find the gate. About that time, I wake up in a cold sweat.

    In the other dream I'm going to the train station. Again, we leave in plenty of time but get stuck in the traffic. I watch the clock as the minutes go by. Finally, the traffic thins, and we begin to move quickly. We arrive at the station with just a few minutes left to catch the train. I run through the station and arrive at the platform just as the train pulls away. This dream never wakes me up.

1. Organize the information about each dream.

   Dream 1　　　　　　　　　　　　　　　**Dream 2**

   _____　　　　　_____

   _____　　　　　_____

   _____　　　　　_____

   _____　　　　　_____

   _____　　　　　_____

   _____　　　　　_____

2. Now compare the information. List two ways that the two dreams are alike.

   a. _____

   _____

   b. _____

   _____

3. Now contrast the information. Write one way that the dreams are different.

   _____

   _____

STRIDES "Twenty-Two," pages 134–145
Comprehension: Comparisons and Contrasts

After you read

Name _____

> **Remember** To make comparisons and contrasts, organize the information about each person, place, or item separately. Then compare and contrast the information.

Follow the directions and write the answers on the lines. Look at the selection if you need help. Some answers are already filled in.

1. Fill in the missing events in Liz's nightmare.
   a. Liz wakes up in the hospital feeling thirsty.
   b. A clock ticks loudly.
   c. She knocks over a glass, and it breaks.
   d. _____
   e. _____
   f. She sees the doors to Room 22.
   g. _____

2. Fill in the events that happen at the airport.
   a. The ticket agent checks Liz in.
   b. _____
   c. Liz feels thirsty.
   d. She hears a clock ticking.
   e. _____
   f. _____
   g. She screams, runs back, and watches the plane explode.

90

STRIDES "Twenty-Two," pages 134–145
Comprehension: Comparisons and Contrasts

Name _____

Now compare and contrast the events.

3. Which events in the nightmare are the same as the events in the airport? Add three more to the list.

   a. *Liz feels thirsty and hears a clock ticking.*

   b. _____

   c. _____

   d. _____

   e. *Liz screams.*

4. In which ways are the nightmare and the incident at the airport different? Add two more to the list.

   a. *There's no airplane in the nightmare.*

   b. _____

   c. _____

5. List one way in which the two women who say "Room for one more" are alike.

   _____

6. List one way in which the two women who say "Room for one more" are different.

   _____

7. Some small similarities between the nightmare and the incident at the airport are never explained. One is given below. Add two more to the list.

   a. *Liz feels thirsty.*

   b. _____

   c. _____

STRIDES "Twenty-Two," pages 134–145
Comprehension: Comparisons and Contrasts

After you read

Name _____

In "Twenty-Two," some of the events are told by the narrator, but most of the information comes from the *dialogue,* or the words the characters say.

A. In the box are ways in which the reader finds out about events from the play "Twenty-Two." On the lines, write the letter or letters of the item or items from the box that answer each question. Look back at the play if you need help.

> A. from the **Narrator**
>
> B. through dialogue between **Liz** and **Nurse 2**
>
> C. through dialogue between the **Doctor** and **Nurse 2**
>
> D. through dialogue between **Liz** and the **Doctor**
>
> E. through dialogue between **Liz** and the **Ticket Agent**

1. Over and over Liz has a nightmare that she cannot explain. In what two ways does the reader find out about the problem? _____ _____

2. The doctor thinks that Liz will not have her nightmare any more after she leaves the hospital. How does the reader find this out? _____

3. The doctor thinks there is something odd about Liz's nightmare. How does the reader find this out? _____

4. Liz goes to the airport. How does the reader find this out? _____

5. Liz's plane is Flight 22. How does the reader find this out? _____

6. Liz screams and runs back to the waiting room. How does the reader find this out? _____

7. The plane takes off and explodes in midair. How does the reader find this out? _____

Name _____

After you read

B. Read the following dialogue between a doctor and a patient in a hospital. Then answer the questions that follow.

> Doctor: Got enough autographs on that cast?
> Patient: I'll get more when I get out of here. They only let a few of my friends in to see me.
> Doctor: Saturday will be here soon enough. Right now, let's check you over.
> Patient: Doc, will I be able to ride my bike again?
> Doctor: Not until you get this cast off your leg.
> Patient: I mean after.
> Doctor: That all depends. Do you mean with or without a hamster cage on the handlebars?
> Patient: Without. I think I've learned my lesson about that!

1. What is wrong with the patient? _____
_____

2. How do you know? _____
_____
_____

3. When will the patient get out of the hospital? _____
_____

4. How was the patient injured? _____
_____
_____
_____

5. What is the patient worried about? _____
_____
_____

STRIDES "Twenty-Two," pages 134–145
Literature: Dialogue

Name _____

The vocabulary words below are from "The Trap." Knowing the words and their meanings will help you understand the selection.

> cardinal   detail   retired

Many words in English have *multiple meanings,* or more than one meaning. Context clues can help the reader decide which meaning a writer has used.

Dictionaries list all the meanings of words. Read the dictionary entries below.

> **car·di·nal** (kär´də·nəl) **1** *adj.* Of first importance; chief. **2** *adj., n.* Deep, rich red. **3** *n.* One of the high officials in the Roman Catholic Church. **4** *n.* A red songbird.
>
> **de·tail** (di·tāl´ or dē´tāl) **1** *n.* A small, secondary part of something. **2** *n.* A minor piece of information. **3** *n.* A small group, as of soldiers or police officers, selected for a special duty.
>
> **re·tire** (ri·tīr´) *v.* re·tired, re·tir·ing **1** To withdraw or remove from a job, often because of age. **2** To go away, as for rest or privacy. **3** To go to bed.

Use the dictionary entries above to determine the meaning of each underlined word as it is used in the sentence. Write the number of the definition on the line.

1. The men watched the cardinal fly from tree to tree. _____

2. We looked at all the red paint and decided that cardinal was the shade of red we wanted to use on the barn. _____

3. That police officer is on the burglary detail. _____

4. Please write and give further details. _____

5. I had been up late three nights in a row, so I retired early last night. _____

6. My grandfather retired from his job when he reached age 65. _____

Name _____

Before you read

Prefixes are word parts that can be added to the beginning of a base or root word. A prefix changes the meaning of the base or root word. Knowing the meanings of word parts can help you understand the meaning of some words.

The prefix *pre-* means "before" or "in advance."
Read the examples.

▶ *Precautions* are *steps taken beforehand* to prevent danger or harm.
▶ If you *prepay*, you *pay in advance*.

A. The following words begin with the prefix *pre-*. Match each word with its definition. Write the letter of the definition on the line where it belongs.

_____ 1. pretest   a. to heat in advance

_____ 2. prearranged   b. before a flight

_____ 3. preschool   c. a test given before studying a subject

_____ 4. preheat   d. before the beginning of school; before school starts

_____ 5. preflight   e. to cook in advance

_____ 6. precook   f. made ready or arranged in advance

B. Write each word from part A in the sentence where it makes sense.

1. Who would've thought that my love for drums since _____ rhythm band would earn me a trip to Washington, D.C.?

2. Our band's trip was _____ by the P.T.A.

3. Before we left, our social studies teacher gave us a _____ on how our government works.

4. I had never flown before, so I got nervous during the flight attendant's _____ instructions before takeoff.

5. It was cold out, so I wondered if the pilot had to _____ the engines.

6. It turned out that everything was great except the food; I think they must _____ it about a week beforehand.

STRIDES   "The Trap," pages 148–159
Vocabulary: Prefixes

95

Name _____

A *conclusion* is a judgment reached by logical thinking. You have learned that as you read a selection, you can draw conclusions about characters. You may also draw conclusions about other things that writers do not state directly.

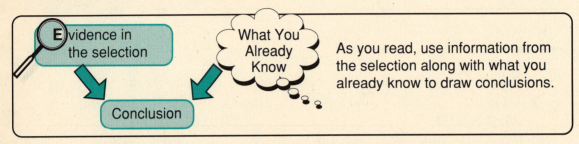

As you read, use information from the selection along with what you already know to draw conclusions.

Read the passage below. Try to draw a conclusion about what James Ritty invented.

James Ritty's restaurant was losing money because some of his cashiers were dishonest. They were not putting all the money into the cash box. James knew what he needed to do to solve the problem. He needed a way to record the amount of money each customer gave the cashier.

While on an ocean trip, James found the answer. In the engine room was a machine that counted and recorded the number of turns the ship's propeller made. When James returned home, he invented a machine which had two rows of keys: one for dollars and one for cents. When the cashier punched the keys to show the amount a customer paid, a dial in the machine recorded that amount.

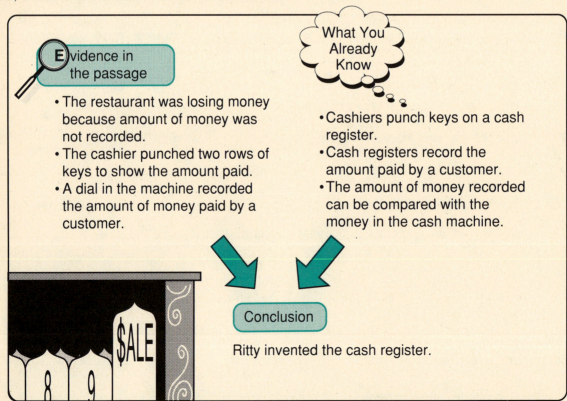

Evidence in the passage
- The restaurant was losing money because amount of money was not recorded.
- The cashier punched two rows of keys to show the amount paid.
- A dial in the machine recorded the amount of money paid by a customer.

What You Already Know
- Cashiers punch keys on a cash register.
- Cash registers record the amount paid by a customer.
- The amount of money recorded can be compared with the money in the cash machine.

Conclusion
Ritty invented the cash register.

STRIDES "The Trap," pages 148–159
Comprehension: Drawing Conclusions

Name _____

Reading Guide

Drawing Conclusions

Follow these steps to draw conclusions as you read:

▶ Think about the evidence in the selection.
▶ Think about what you already know.
▶ Combine the evidence and your own knowledge to draw a conclusion about what is happening and why.

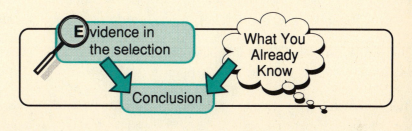

A. As you read the paragraph, think about the evidence in the passage and about what you already know. Read the questions and the answers.

A.   This is one version of a delicious invention. It was a hot day at the World's Fair in 1904 in St. Louis. Abe Doumar was selling souvenirs. As he worked, he overheard an ice cream seller talking about a problem. The ice cream seller had plenty of ice cream, but he had run out of dishes. Abe had a solution. He told the ice cream seller to fold waffles into funnel shapes and to fill them with ice cream. The ice cream man tried Abe's idea. Soon people were running to the ice cream stand to buy the new treat.

1. What did Abe Doumar invent to solve the problem? Circle the answer.
   waffle iron   (ice cream cone)   ice cream bar

2. What evidence in the selection did you use to draw your conclusion? _Doumar told the ice cream man to fill funnel-shaped waffles with ice cream._

3. What is one fact you already knew that helped you draw your conclusion? _I knew that ice cream cones are funnel shaped and taste somewhat like waffles._

STRIDES "The Trap," pages 148–159
Comprehension: Drawing Conclusions

Name _____

B. **Read the paragraph. Then read the questions and circle the answers or write your answers on the lines.**

In the 1890's, every piece of clothing was fastened with buttons. It took a lot of time to fasten all the buttons on boots, shoes, pants, dresses, shirts, and skirts. Then Whitcomb Judson thought of a way to save time for everyone. He made a quick fastener, using two thin metal chains with a slider between them. The chains fastened when the slider was pulled. At first, Whitcomb's solution to the button problem was used just for shoes and boots. Later, it was used on just about every kind of clothing.

1. What did Whitcomb Judson invent? Circle the answer.
   shoe horn   boot hook   zipper

2. What evidence in the selection did you use to draw your conclusion?
   _____
   _____
   _____

3. What is one fact you already knew that helped you draw your conclusion?
   _____

C. **Think about the strategies you used to answer the questions in part B. Then read the paragraph and answer the questions.**

Levi Hutchins's job began early in the morning. To be on time, Levi had to get up at 4:00 A.M., so it's not surprising that he often overslept. Luckily, Levi was a clockmaker. His clocks gave him the solution to his problem. Levi added a gear to one of his clocks. Each morning at 4:00, the minute hand of the clock tripped the gear. The gear started a bell ringing, which woke Levi up.

1. What did Levi Hutchins invent? Circle the answer.
   telephone bell   alarm clock   cuckoo clock

2. What evidence in the selection did you use to draw your conclusion?
   _____
   _____

3. What is one fact you already knew that helped you draw your conclusion?
   _____

STRIDES "The Trap," pages 148–159
Comprehension: Drawing Conclusions

Name _____

After you read

Remember A *conclusion* is a judgment reached by logical thinking. To draw a conclusion, use evidence in the selection along with what you already know.

As you read "The Trap," you were probably able to draw a conclusion about the solution to the crime and how the crime was committed before you finished the story. If you did, you based your conclusions on evidence in the story and on what you already knew. Follow the directions to write about your conclusions.

1. On page 155 Cissy says, "I just solved my case." At this point in the story, the reader has enough clues to solve the crimes. Write the evidence from the story that helped you draw a conclusion about the solution to the crimes. You may list facts, events, or things people said. Reread pages 151–155 of the story if you need help.

    a. _____
    _____

    b. _____
    _____

    c. _____
    _____

2. The last two paragraphs of the story explain how the burglars committed their crimes. Before you get to these paragraphs, however, you have enough evidence to figure it out on your own. List the information that you knew that you combined with the evidence to help you conclude how the burglars committed the crimes.

    a. _____
    _____

    b. _____
    _____

    c. _____
    _____

STRIDES "The Trap," pages 148–159
Comprehension: Drawing Conclusions

After you read

Name _____

The *Yellow Pages* are the part of a telephone directory that lists businesses. The alphabetical headings describe people and companies that sell products and services. Many directories include an index to help you select the correct heading. The *Yellow Page* listings may also contain some information that may help you decide which company or person to call. By using the *Yellow Pages*, you can find the telephone number and address of the company or person that can help you.

Study the example from the *Yellow Pages* and the notes.

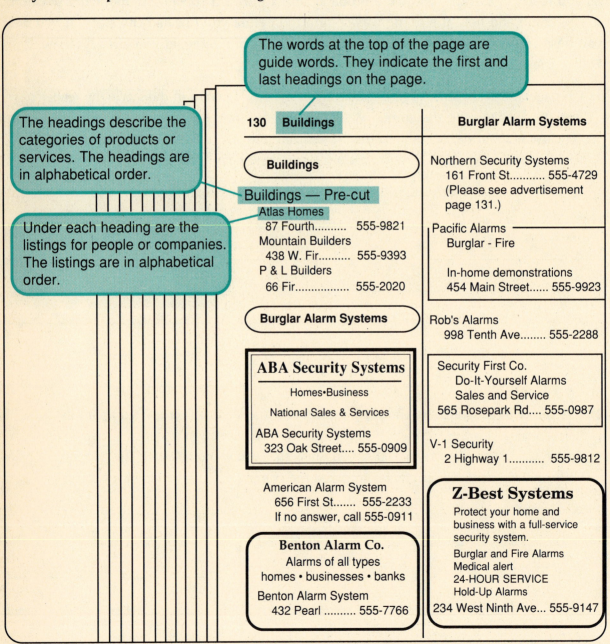

STRIDES "The Trap," pages 148–159
Study Skills: Reference Sources—Telephone Book

Name _____

Use the *Yellow Page* on Study Guide page 100 to answer the questions below. Write the answers on the lines.

1. After the robbery, Mrs. Cardinal decided to buy an alarm system for her home. In the index for the *Yellow Pages* under *Alarms,* she found the following listings:

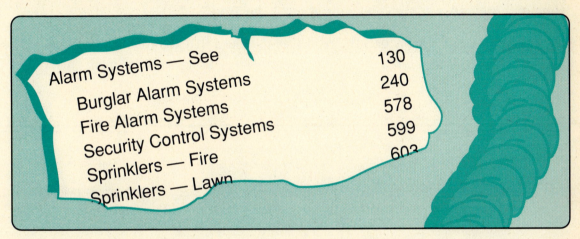

   On what page of the *Yellow Pages* should she look to find listings for burglar alarms?
   _____

2. On page 130, Mrs. Cardinal found several companies listed. The first one she called was American Alarm System. No one answered the phone when she dialed 555-2233. What number should she dial next?
   _____

3. As Mrs. Cardinal scanned the other listings on the page, she saw one for a company that gives demonstrations in the home. Which company is that?
   _____

   What is the address? _____

4. While scanning the page, she also noticed that one company sells alarms that people can install themselves. Which company sells such alarms?
   _____

5. A friend told Mrs. Cardinal that Northern Security Systems had a very good service record. She looked up their number. She realized that she wanted more information about the company before she called. Where might she get that information?
   _____

STRIDES   "The Trap," pages 148–159
Study Skills: Reference Sources—Telephone Book

Name _____

A *mystery* is a form of fiction in which a puzzling or an unusual event occurs. Detective stories such as "The Trap" are one type of mystery. In a detective story a crime is committed, and a detective tries to figure out who committed it.

Mystery writers follow certain guidelines when they write their stories. Read each guideline and then answer the questions about "The Trap."

1. Good mystery writers usually give the reader all the clues that the main character has. The writer does this so that the reader can solve the mystery along with the main character.

   Does the writer of "The Trap" give you all the clues that Cissy has?
   _____ If no, what clues does she keep from you? _____
   _____

2. Good mystery writers have the main character solve the mystery by gathering evidence and thinking logically about it.

   Give one example of how Cissy uses clues and logical thinking to solve the mystery of the crime. _____

3. Good mystery writers make the solution to the mystery believable.

   Do you think the solution in "The Trap" is believable? _____
   Explain why or why not. _____
   _____

4. Sometimes a writer gives misleading clues to make the mystery more confusing.

   Does the writer of "The Trap" use this technique? _____ If yes, what misleading clues does she give? _____
   _____

5. To keep you interested, good mystery writers keep you involved in the story by giving you the same clues that they give the main character.

   Did you try to solve the mystery along with Cissy? _____
   _____
   If yes, did you solve the mystery before the writer told you the solution? _____
   _____

Name _____

Before you read

The vocabulary words below are from "Daring Mission." Knowing the words and their meanings will help you understand the selection.

> betrayed   patriots   quarters
> rejoiced   seized   stern   translate

Context clues are the other words and phrases that help you understand an unfamiliar word in a sentence or a paragraph.

A. Read each sentence. Use context clues to help you decide what the underlined word means. Circle the letter in front of the best answer. Then underline the context clues you used to help you figure out the word's meaning.

1. The American patriots fought the British because they loved America and wanted to make it free from British rule.

   In the sentence, *patriots* means people who _____.
   a. dislike their country
   b. fight for any country
   c. cannot be trusted
   d. love and defend their country

2. When the British took over Americans' homes, they also seized the Americans' horses and supplies.

   In the sentence, *seized* means _____.
   a. took over by force
   b. fed and cared for
   c. gave to
   d. enjoyed greatly

3. Sometimes a spy would carefully translate secret messages from a code into English.

   In the sentence, *translate* means _____.
   a. write very lightly
   b. turn into another language
   c. trade for money
   d. carry a long way

4. A person's words may sound stern if he or she speaks in a very firm voice.

   In the sentence, *stern* means _____.
   a. friendly   b. sweet   c. harsh   d. quiet

5. The soldiers' families were extremely happy and rejoiced when the soldiers returned safely.

   In the sentence, *rejoiced* means _____.
   a. expressed gladness
   b. felt sorry
   c. were upset
   d. relaxed

STRIDES "Daring Mission," pages 162–173
Vocabulary: Context Clues

Name _____

6. The infamous American traitor Benedict Arnold betrayed his country by sending secret information to an enemy general in the British army.

   In the sentence, *betrayed* means _____.
   a. loved and honored
   b. helped the enemy of
   c. took over by force
   d. fought for

7. The soldiers' quarters on the army base were all in large buildings that looked like apartment houses.

   In the sentence, *quarters* means _____.
   a. 25 cents in coins
   b. parts of a football game
   c. a square divided into four parts
   d. a place where someone lives

B. Read the paragraph. Fill in the blanks using words from the box on page 103. Not all of the words will be used.

Nathan Hale was one of the _____ who fought to help America win freedom from British rule. He was excited about American independence, and he _____ when he had a chance to help. In September 1776, Hale agreed to obtain some secret information for General George Washington. Before Hale could give the information to Washington, he was _____ by British soldiers and taken to the British general. With a _____ and unsmiling face, the British general declared that Nathan Hale must die. Even then, Hale was loyal and never _____ America to the enemy.

STRIDES "Daring Mission," pages 162–173
Vocabulary: Context Clues

Name _____

Synonyms are words that have the same or almost the same meaning. *Antonyms* are words that have opposite meanings.

A. Read each sentence. Notice the underlined word. From the box, choose a synonym for the word. Write it on the line to complete the sentence.

| rooms | hurrying | pieces | work | harsh |

1. Eric didn't mind doing chores, so he was happy to find summer _____ clearing hiking trails.

2. For six weeks, he shared two large _____ in the rangers' quarters with other young men.

3. The chief forest ranger looked stern, but he was not a _____ man.

4. He was rushing to get the trails open by August, so he kept the young men _____ all day.

5. At suppertime, Eric ate the stew of _____ of vegetables and chunks of meat as if it were a feast.

B. Read each sentence. Notice the underlined word. Choose an antonym for the word from the box. Write it on the line to complete the sentence.

| listened | awake | help | leave | traitor |

1. If it was hard to fall asleep, there was always someone else _____ in the rangers' quarters.

2. Often late at night, Eric _____ as his new friend Trevor told stories of his life in urban Boston.

3. Eric, descended from an American patriot, learned that Trevor's long-dead relative had been a _____.

4. As their friendship grew, it became natural to _____ one another and to protect one another from harm.

5. When it was time to _____ camp and return to the city, both of the young men wished they could stay.

STRIDES "Daring Mission," pages 162–173
Vocabulary: Synonyms and Antonyms

Name _____

Time clue words and phrases help the reader recognize and remember the *sequence,* or order, of events in a selection. Time clue words also help the reader decide how much time has passed between events in the selection.

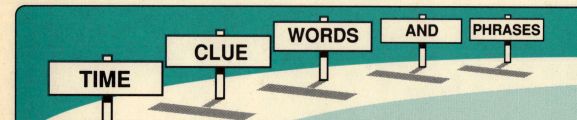

Tell *when* an event happens:

| in 1776 | yesterday | next | tonight |
| on Tuesday | the next day | first | finally |

Tell *how much* time has passed or *how long* something lasts:

for a month   two years later

for two weeks   in a few hours

The American Revolution began on April 19, 1775, when British soldiers clashed with American colonists at Lexington, Massachusetts. At nearby Concord, just a few hours later, the "shot heard 'round the world" began the second battle of the eight-year war.

When did it begin?

When did the next event happen?

How long did it last?

Reading Guide

Using Time Clues to Sequence Events

As you read, use these tips to help you understand the sequence of events:

▶ Try to recognize and remember the sequence of events by asking yourself, "*When* does this event happen?"

▶ Decide how much time has passed by asking yourself, "*How much* time has passed?"

STRIDES "Daring Mission," pages 162–173
Comprehension: Sequence—Time Clues

Name _____

A. As you read the paragraph, think about the order of events. Then read the questions and the answers.

 In 1776 the Revolution did not go well for the Americans. First, the British occupied New York, and General George Washington's army had to retreat. The American army grew smaller and smaller as the months passed. By the end of the year, Washington was desperate. He felt that the war might end in defeat in only ten more days.

1. What words tell *how long* something has been going on?

   as the months passed

2. What words tell *when* something happened or will happen?

   in 1776, first, by the end of the year, in only ten more days

B. Read the paragraph. Then read the questions and write your answers on the lines.

 On Christmas night Washington's troops crossed the Delaware River in a surprise attack on Trenton, New Jersey. A short time later the troops defending Trenton surrendered. Finally the Americans had won an important victory. At once, many more soldiers signed up to join in a struggle for independence that would continue for four more years.

1. What words tell *how long* something has been going on?

   _____

2. What words tell *when* something happened?

   _____

C. Think about the strategies you used to answer the questions in part B. Then read the paragraph and answer the questions.

 The next spring the British attacked from Canada. Fighting continued for months until the British under General Burgoyne surrendered in October. Philadelphia was captured by the British in September 1777. They controlled the city for nine months.

1. What words tell *how long* something has been going on?

   _____

2. What words tell *when* something happened?

   _____

STRIDES "Daring Mission," pages 162–173
Comprehension: Sequence—Time Clues

Name _____

Sequence is the order in which the events in a selection happen. **Time clues** are words and phrases that help the reader recognize and remember the order of events. Use time clues to help you decide *when* an event occurs and *how much* time passes between events.

A. Fill in the missing events in the order in which they happened in the story "Daring Mission." Use the time clues for help.

1. On a December afternoon, _____.

2. As the British officers meet, *Lydia overhears them plan an attack on General Washington's forces.*

3. That night after the meeting, _____.

4. The following morning, _____.

5. After his meeting with Lydia, *Colonel Craig promises to get her message to General Washington.*

6. Two days later, _____.

7. Four days later, _____.

8. That afternoon, _____.

9. When she is questioned, *Lydia convinces the British of her innocence, and they let her go.*

Name _____

B. Read each question. Write the answers on the lines.

1. Scan part 2 of "Daring Mission." List four time clues in that part of the selection.
   _____
   _____
   _____
   _____

2. When does Lydia leave for Frankford? _____
   _____

3. How long does it take her to deliver her message and return to Philadelphia? _____
   _____

4. How much time passes between Lydia's delivery of her message and the British army's march out of Philadelphia to attack the American army?
   _____

5. How long are the British troops gone? _____
   _____

6. When does the British officer call Lydia in for questioning? _____
   _____

Name _____

Maps often use symbols to give information. The map *legend* explains each symbol.

Study the map below. It shows the thirteen original colonies that fought the British in the Revolutionary War. It also includes symbols that show where important battles of the war took place.

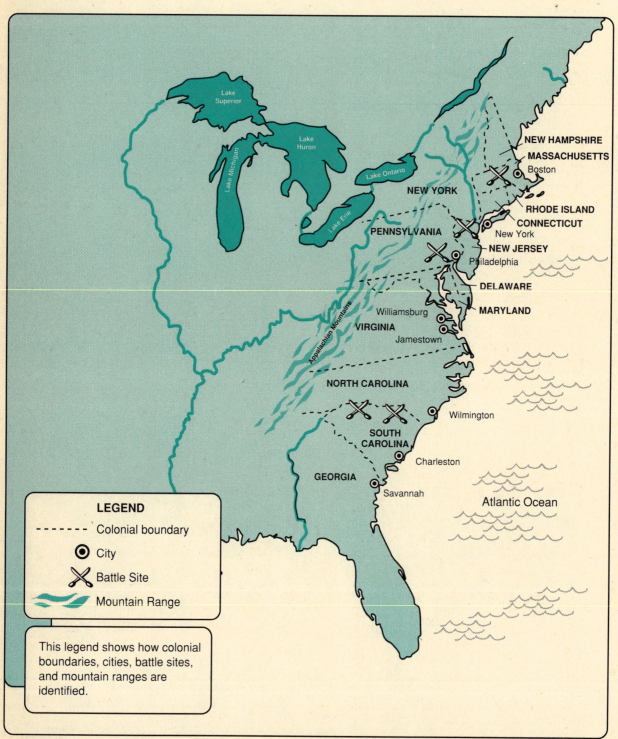

Name _____

Use the map on Study Guide page 110 to answer the questions below. Circle the letter in front of the correct answer, or write the answer on the lines.

1. What is the symbol for a colonial boundary?
   a. ～～　　b. - - - - - -　　c. ⚔

2. What does ⊙ stand for?
   a. a battle site　　b. a city　　c. a country's boundary

3. Which of these is the name of a city?
   a. Philadelphia　　b. Virginia　　c. Connecticut

4. Which of these is the name of a colony?
   a. Boston　　b. New Hampshire　　c. Savannah

5. One mountain range is shown on the map. What is the name of the mountain range?
   _____

6. Five lakes are shown on the map. What are their names?
   _____
   _____

7. In "Daring Mission," Lydia Darragh lives in Philadelphia. In what colony is Philadelphia?
   _____

8. What city in South Carolina is shown on the map? _____

9. Near what city in Massachusetts was a battle fought? _____

10. List the names of five of the original colonies. Use the map for help.
    _____
    _____
    _____

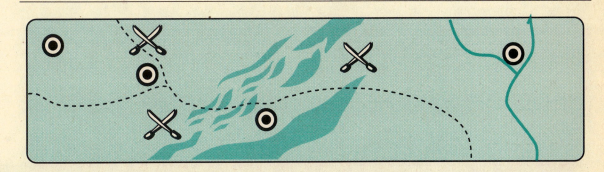

STRIDES "Daring Mission," pages 162–173
Study Skills: Map Legend

111

Name _____

The *setting* is the time and place in which events occur. "Daring Mission" takes place during an important time in America's history, the American Revolution. Sometimes knowing about historical events can help a reader understand a selection.

A. Read each question about the historical setting of "Daring Mission." Write the answers on the lines. Use your reading book for help.

1. In what year does "Daring Mission" take place? _____

2. Where does "Daring Mission" take place? _____

3. How does knowing that the British controlled Philadelphia help the reader understand the events in "Daring Mission"? _____
_____
_____

B. Think about the historical setting of "Daring Mission." On the lines, describe *when* and *where* the following parts of the story happen. Use details from part 1 of the selection to describe each setting.

1. the conversation between Lydia and the British officer when he tells her that there will be a meeting at her house _____
_____
_____

2. the meeting of the British officers to plan the attack on Washington's army _____
_____
_____
_____

3. the last paragraph of part 1 _____
_____
_____
_____

112

STRIDES "Daring Mission," pages 162–173
Literature: Setting

Name _____

After you read

C. On the lines below, describe *when* and *where* the following parts of the story happen. Use details from part 2 of the selection to describe each setting.

1. The first paragraph of part 2 _____
   _____

2. Lydia's meeting with Colonel Craig _____
   _____
   _____

3. the British officer's questioning of Lydia after the British troops are betrayed _____
   _____
   _____

4. the end of the story _____
   _____

D. Use the answers to the questions in part C to fill in the chart below. The first section has been done for you.

PART OF THE STORY	WHEN	WHERE
the first paragraph of part 2	the next morning, a bright, bitter cold day	Philadelphia
Lydia's meeting with Colonel Craig		
the British officer's questioning of Lydia		
the end of the story		

STRIDES "Daring Mission," pages 162–173
Literature: Setting

Name _____

One common type of item on a test is one from which a word has been left out of a sentence. Your job as a test taker is to choose the best word from a group of words to complete the sentence. Using an organized strategy makes it easier to answer this type of test item correctly.

Study the sample item, strategy steps, and notes.

A student must take math or another required _____ in order to be graduated.

- **A** read
- **B** television
- **C** course
- **D** country

1 Read the test items. Before reading the possible answers, think of a word that makes sense in the sentence. The word you use may not be the right answer, but it will probably be similar in meaning.

The word *subject* fits into the sentence.

2 Look at all of the answers. You may immediately find a word that is close in meaning to the word you thought of. However, it may not be the best answer. To avoid making a quick and incorrect choice, read all of the answer choices. Quickly eliminate the ones that don't make sense and are obviously wrong.

Immediately eliminate *read* and *television*. *Read* is an action word, and the missing word is one that answers the question *"what."* *Television* is not studied in school. There are two choices left: *course* and *country*. Both answer the question *"what."*

3 To choose the best and correct answer, try each remaining choice in the sentence to see which makes sense. Use the context clues in the sentence to help you.

Try *country* and *course* in the sentence. Since *math* is not an example of a country, *country* cannot be the correct answer. *Course* is the correct answer.

STRIDES "Trombones and Colleges," pages 174–187
Study Skills: Test-Taking Strategies

Name _____

> **Reading Guide**
>
> **Using Test-Taking Strategies**
> When answering a sentence completion item, follow these steps:
>
> ▶ Read the item and think of a word that fits.
> ▶ Read all the answer choices. Eliminate the ones that don't fit in the sentence. Use context clues and word parts to find out the meanings of any unfamiliar words.
> ▶ Try each possible choice in the sentence to determine which is best. Use context clues to help you decide.

A. Use the three-step strategy to answer the test items below. Follow the directions.

1. Read the test item.

   | The principal decided to _____ the classrooms green. |

   a. What is one word that makes sense in the sentence? _____
      What kind of word must the answer be to fit into the sentence? Fill in the answer circle.
      - Ⓐ an action word
      - Ⓑ a word that describes
      - Ⓒ a word that tells where
      - Ⓓ a word that tells who or what

   b. Now read the test item and the answer choices.

   | The principal decided to _____ the classroom green. |
   | Ⓐ beautiful   Ⓒ clean |
   | Ⓑ blue   Ⓓ paint |

   Which two answer choices can you eliminate immediately, and why?

   _____ because _____

   _____ because _____

   Try the sentence again, using the choices that are left. Fill in the circle in front of the best answer.

   How do you know that it is the best answer? _____

   c. Put a check in the box to rate your response to **a**. The best answer to the test item is ___.
      - ☐ the same word I thought of in **a**
      - ☐ similar in meaning to the word I thought of in **a**
      - ☐ not close to the meaning of the word I thought of in **a**

STRIDES "Trombones and Colleges," pages 174–187
Study Skills: Test-Taking Strategies

Name _____

2. Read the test item.

> Her face became _____ when she heard the terrible news.

a. What is one word that makes sense in the sentence? _____
What kind of word must the answer be to fit in the sentence? Fill in the answer circle.
- Ⓐ an action word
- Ⓑ a word that describes
- Ⓒ a word that tells where
- Ⓓ a word that tells who or what

b. Now read the test item and the answer choices.

> Her face became _____ when she heard the terrible news.
> Ⓐ happy   Ⓑ cried   Ⓒ red   Ⓓ pale

Which two answer choices can you eliminate immediately, and why?

_____ because _____

_____ because _____

Try the sentence again, using the choices that are left. Fill in the circle in front of the best answer.

How do you know that it is the best answer? _____

c. Put a check in the box to rate your response to **a**. The best answer to the test item is _____.
- ☐ the same word I thought of in **a**.
- ☐ similar in meaning to the word I thought of in **a**.
- ☐ not close to the meaning of the word I thought of in **a**.

B. Now use the strategy for the following items. Read each item. Fill in the circle in front of the word that best completes the sentence.

1. It was difficult to choose which _____ to play in the band.
- Ⓐ sing
- Ⓑ instrument
- Ⓒ football
- Ⓓ loud

2. Taylor worked hard to learn to _____ the piano.
- Ⓐ play
- Ⓑ guitar
- Ⓒ paint
- Ⓓ tuneful

3. Now I can play every _____ in the book.
- Ⓐ study
- Ⓑ class
- Ⓒ difficult
- Ⓓ song

Name _____

Before you read

The vocabulary words below are from "Trombones and Colleges." Knowing the words and their meanings will help you understand the selection.

Read the words and their definitions.

academic:	having to do with general education rather than job or business training
adviser:	a teacher who gives students advice about studies and careers
commercial:	having to do with preparing students for jobs in business
nonchalant:	seeming not excited or concerned
pawn shop:	a store where a person borrows money and leaves an object of value as security
transformers:	devices that increase or decrease the voltage of electrical current

Use the definitions above to help you choose the word that best completes each sentence. Also use the test-taking strategies you have learned to help you choose the correct answer. Fill in the circle in front of the best answer.

1. Kate talked with her _____ about what classes she should take next year in high school.

    Ⓐ summer school   Ⓑ grades   Ⓒ adviser   Ⓓ academic

2. Mr. Paul left his gold watch at the _____ so he could borrow some money.

    Ⓐ transformers   Ⓑ office   Ⓒ nonchalant   Ⓓ pawn shop

3. Since Jason wanted to go to college, he chose the _____ program when he entered high school.

    Ⓐ elective   Ⓑ adviser   Ⓒ academic   Ⓓ commercial

4. A course in doing office work is part of our school's _____ program.

    Ⓐ commercial   Ⓑ college   Ⓒ academic   Ⓓ mathematics

5. The power company must use _____ in order to provide electricity.

    Ⓐ transformers   Ⓑ gasoline   Ⓒ commercial   Ⓓ manufacture

6. Even though Keith acted _____, he was really worried about the test.

    Ⓐ anxiety   Ⓑ nonchalant   Ⓒ rejoiced   Ⓓ adviser

STRIDES "Trombones and Colleges," pages 174–187
Vocabulary: Word Meanings

Name _____

An author always has a *purpose*, or reason, for writing.

The author's purpose may be to inform, to entertain, to persuade.

PURPOSES

A trombone is a brass musical instrument. The player blows into the mouthpiece. When this happens, the air moves through the tube and out at the bell. To play a lower or a higher note, the trombonist moves the slide back and forth.

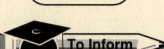
To Inform
The author gives information about a topic. The selection mostly contains facts.

It didn't take long for Steve to discover that playing the trombone was not as easy as it looked. First, his cheeks puffed out like a chipmunk's. Try as he might, he could not make a sound come out of the instrument. Soon Steve's face was as red as a traffic light. He huffed and puffed, and finally, "Blaaaat!" sputtered the trombone. "I'm a musician!" Steve cried.

To Entertain
The author gives descriptions and tells a story with people and events to create feelings in the reader. Feelings may range from enjoyment to terror.

Any person who wants to be a serious musician should learn to play the trombone. Because the trombone is such an important instrument, it is used in bands and orchestras everywhere. People who cannot play the trombone cannot claim to be true musicians.

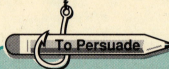
To Persuade
An author may give an opinion and try to make you believe the same thing he or she does. Often an author will support the opinion with facts.

Sometimes an author may have more than one purpose for writing a selection.

STRIDES "Trombones and Colleges," pages 174–187
Comprehension: Author's Purpose

Name _____

Identifying the Author's Purpose

As you read, pay attention to the author's purpose.

Ask Yourself: Does the writer give factual information about a topic?

Ask Yourself: Does the writer entertain by creating feelings?

Ask Yourself: Is the writer trying to persuade me to believe something?

▶ Remember that a writer may have more than one purpose for writing a selection.

A. As you read the paragraph, look for evidence to help you identify the author's purpose. Then read the questions and the answers.

   Did you know that I played in the band when I was in high school? I played the trumpet, and it was fun except during football season. Then we would all sit in the stands, blowing our lungs out to cheer on the team. At every single game, we trumpets had to sit right in front of the trombones. Can you imagine having a herd of charging elephants right behind you? That's just about how loud those trombones sounded. Every player tried to be louder than the next. It wasn't just the noise that bothered us, though. Have you seen how a trombone works? To make a low note, the player pushes the slide WAY out. Every time those slides would go out, they would poke us in our backs. I think the trombone players had a contest to see which one could make the most bruises on a trumpet player's back. The trombonist behind me won, every time!

1. What is the author's main purpose? _to entertain_

2. How do you know? _The author gives descriptions and tells a story with events to create feelings of enjoyment in the reader._

STRIDES "Trombones and Colleges," pages 174–187
Comprehension: Author's Purpose

Name _____

B. Read the paragraph. Then read the questions and write your answers on the lines.

If you would like to be in the high school band, you should begin taking trombone lessons. Why should you choose the trombone as your instrument? First, it is an important instrument that plays a major part in the band. Who could imagine a marching band without trombones? Second, a trombone is fun to play. No other instrument changes notes when a slide is pushed out and pulled in. I think doing that is much more interesting than beating a drum. Third, good trombone players are always in demand. Many players take up the trombone, but few become really good at it. This leads to the second part of my advice: You should begin your lessons right now. The more you learn as a beginner, the more quickly you will advance to more difficult music. Then you will probably have a better chance of becoming a top player.

1. What is the author's main purpose? _____

2. How do you know? _____

_____

_____

C. Think about the strategies you used to answer the questions in part B. Then read the paragraph and answer the questions.

The trombone is a member of the brass family of musical instruments. Every brass instrument has a mouthpiece at one end and a bell-shaped opening at the other. Most brass instruments have valves that the player presses in order to play a higher or a lower note. Trombones, however, have either slides or valves. Unlike woodwind instruments such as the clarinet or saxophone, brass instruments do not use reeds to produce sounds. Instead, the player vibrates his or her lips while blowing into the mouthpiece. Making the lips tighter or looser helps the player control the pitch of the sound being played.

1. What is the author's main purpose? _____

2. How do you know? _____

_____

_____

Name _____

> An author has a purpose for writing a selection. The purpose may be . . .
>
>
>
> An author may have more than one purpose for writing.

Answer the questions below about "Trombones and Colleges." Write the answers on the lines.

1. Reread the passage on page 178 in which Clyde tells about talking with the grade adviser. What feeling does the author create in this paragraph? _____
_____

2. Reread the paragraph on page 181 in which Clyde begins to smile even though he still has tears in his eyes. What feeling does the author create in this paragraph? _____
_____

3. Reread the passage on pages 182–185 about the time that Clyde's father tried to learn to play the trombone. What feeling does the author create in this passage? _____
_____

4. Reread the last two paragraphs of the story. What feeling does the author create in this passage? _____
_____

5. What is the author's main purpose in writing "Trombones and Colleges"? _____
_____

6. Does the author achieve his purpose? _____ Explain why you think he does or does not. _____
_____
_____

STRIDES "Trombones and Colleges," pages 174–187
Comprehension: Author's Purpose

Name _____

Trombones and Colleges

Imagine that "Trombones and Colleges" is a book and that you are working for its publisher. Your job is to write the information that appears on the inside flaps of the book jacket.

← **On this inside flap your purpose is to inform. You are to tell the reader what the book is about.**

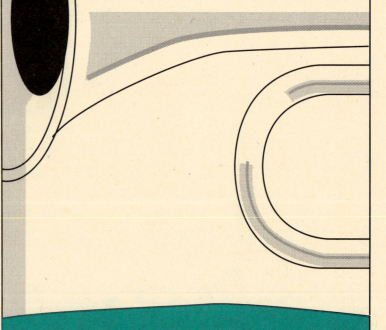

122   **STRIDES** "Trombones and Colleges," pages 174–187
Language: Writing for Different Purposes

Name _____

After you read

On the other inside flap, your purpose is to persuade someone to buy the book. You must try to convince whoever reads the flap that the book is worth reading.

STRIDES "Trombones and Colleges," pages 174–187
Language: Writing for Different Purposes

123

Name _____

The vocabulary words below are from "Treasure Beneath the Sea." Knowing the words and their meanings will help you understand the selection.

Read the words and their definitions.

> coral: a stony substance formed from the skeletons of tiny sea animals
>
> documents: written or printed papers that give official information
>
> fleet: a group of ships sailing under one person's command
>
> hurricane: a storm with heavy rains and very strong winds
>
> metal detector: a tool that discovers anything made of metal
>
> murky: dark or gloomy
>
> reefs: ridges of sand, rocks, or coral starting on the ocean bottom and often rising to the surface

Use the definitions above to help you choose the word that completes each sentence. Fill in the circle in front of the best answer.

1. When we visited Hawaii, we went scuba diving in the shallow waters of the coral _____.

   Ⓐ current   Ⓑ murky   Ⓒ undertow   Ⓓ reefs

2. The _____ was due to sail into the bay at noon.

   Ⓐ fleet   Ⓑ coral   Ⓒ ride   Ⓓ departing

3. Someone was using a _____ to find money that sunbathers had lost in the sand.

   Ⓐ metal detector   Ⓑ adviser   Ⓒ diver   Ⓓ documents

4. After the storm, the water was too _____ for the divers to see each other.

   Ⓐ coral   Ⓑ clear   Ⓒ exhausted   Ⓓ murky

5. The winds of the _____ blew off rooftops and knocked over trees.

   Ⓐ gushed   Ⓑ metal detector   Ⓒ twilight   Ⓓ hurricane

6. Mrs. Chen keeps all important _____, such as her will, in a locked file.

   Ⓐ reefs   Ⓑ documents   Ⓒ detail   Ⓓ safety

7. The reefs around the Hawaiian Islands are formed of brightly colored _____.

   Ⓐ fish   Ⓑ ash   Ⓒ coral   Ⓓ fleet

Name _____

Homophones are words that sound the same but are spelled differently and have different meanings. You must use the correct homophone in your writing so that your readers will understand what you mean.

A. Read the sets of homophones and their meanings. Use them to fill in the correct homophones in the sentences. Not all of the words will be used.

SOUND THE SAME

weak	not strong	heard	listened
week	seven days	herd	a group of animals
beech	a kind of tree	sun	a star
beach	a seashore	son	a male child
sail	to travel by boat	sea	ocean
sale	a reduction of prices	see	look

DIFFERENT MEANINGS

1. After having the flu, he felt too _____ (weak, week) to join his shipmates on the voyage.

2. The ship will _____ (sail, sale) for Florida tomorrow.

3. For three days, the _____ (sun, son) shone and a steady breeze blew.

4. We _____ (heard, herd) the rain pounding on the decks.

5. The ship had been at _____ (sea, see) for three days.

6. The entire voyage will take a whole _____ (weak, week).

7. The captain of the ship has a _____ (sun, son) and two daughters.

8. As we sailed close to the _____ (beech, beach), we could _____ (sea, see) the coral reefs just beneath the surface of the water.

B. Now write a sentence in which you use one pair of homophones. Be sure to use each of the homophones in the correct way.

Example: She felt *weak* after being sick for a whole *week*.

_____

_____

STRIDES "Treasure Beneath the Sea," pages 190–207
Vocabulary: Homophones

Name _____

A *cause-and-effect relationship* shows how one event leads to another.

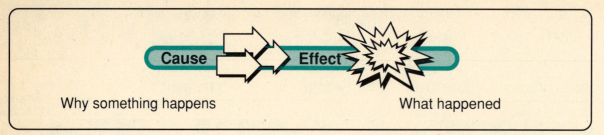

Sometimes there may be more than one effect, or more than one thing that happened.

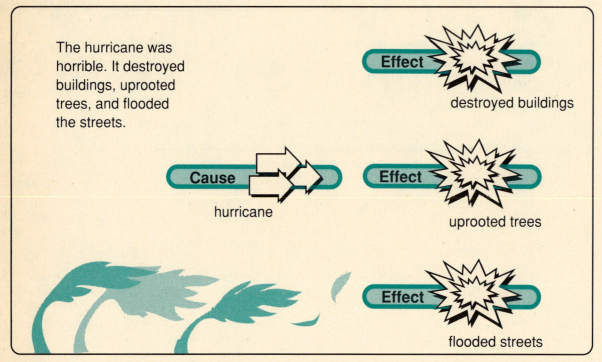

Sometimes there may be more than one cause of an event.

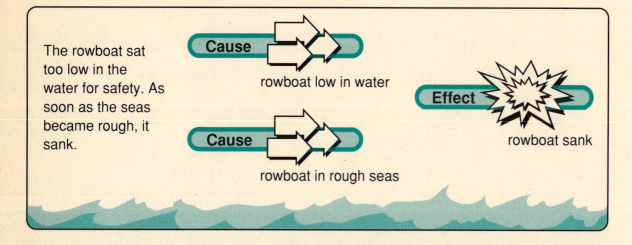

Name _____

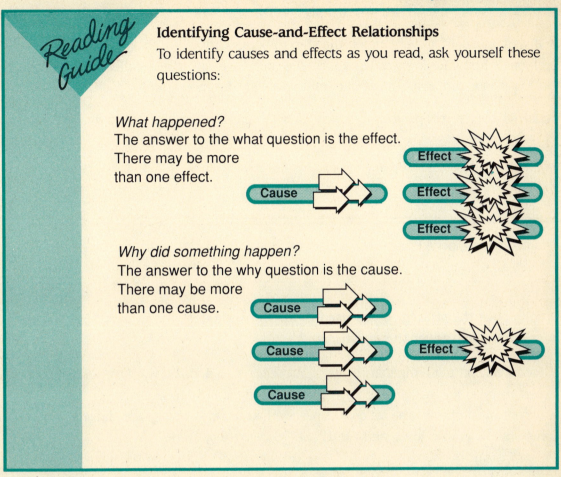

A. As you read the passage, identify the cause and the effects. Then read the questions and the answers.

The snowstorm caused all kinds of problems. Traffic was tied up for hours, and the power went off. I also read that the airport was closed for the day.

1. Cause: Why did the problems happen? _The problems happened because of the snowstorm._

2. Effect: What happened? List three effects on the lines below.

   a. _Traffic was tied up for hours._
   b. _The power went off._
   c. _The airport was closed for the day._

STRIDES "Treasure Beneath the Sea," pages 190–207
Comprehension: Multiple Causes and Effects

Name _____

B. Read the paragraph. Then read the questions, and write your answers on the lines.

It was unusual for everyone on the ship to be so jumpy. We finally figured out that everyone's funny feeling was caused by the quiet seas and hot weather. The strange looking clouds probably had something to do with the mood, too.

1. *Cause*: Why were people feeling jumpy? List three causes on the lines below.

   a. _____

   b. _____

   c. _____

2. *Effect*: What happened that was so unusual? _____
   _____

C. Think about the strategies you used to answer the questions in part B. Then read the paragraph and answer the questions.

Last weekend the temperatures were below freezing and the wind were strong. The streets were so icy that driving anywhere was dangerous. Because of the bad weather, we spent most of our time indoors. Since we had to stay inside, Mom finished building some shelves in my closet, and I read two good mystery stories.

1. *Cause*: Why were people indoors? _____

2. *Effect*: What happened because of the weather? List three effects on the lines below.

   a. _____

   b. _____

   c. _____

As the tree fell, it did a great deal of damage. It knocked down power lines and blocked the road. It also hit a deer and killed it.

3. *Cause*: Why was there damage? _____

4. *Effect*: What happened? List three effects on the lines below.

   a. _____

   b. _____

   c. _____

STRIDES "Treasure Beneath the Sea," pages 190–207
Comprehension: Multiple Causes and Effects

Name _____

After you read

 **Remember** The *cause* is the reason something happens. It comes first in time. There may be more than one cause of an event. An *effect* is the result of a cause. A cause may have more than one effect.

Read each question and write your answers on the lines. Go back to the selection if you need help.

1. What *effect* did the general's decision to head for Spain have on the fleet?
   _____
   _____

2. On the fourth day at sea, the sailors began to worry. What three signs *caused* them to worry?

   a. _____

   b. _____

   c. _____

3. What *caused* the Spanish ships to sink? _____
   _____

4. What two events *caused* Kip to become interested in the sunken treasure?

   a. _____

   b. _____

5. What two problems *caused* the divers to grumble on that February morning in 1961?

   a. _____
   _____

   b. _____
   _____

6. What was the *result* of Kip's search for sunken treasure? _____
   _____

STRIDES "Treasure Beneath the Sea," pages 190–207
Comprehension: Multiple Causes and Effects

Name _____

Reference sources provide information. To find information on a subject or to verify information you have, use reference sources.

Read the list of reference books below. The list tells what each type of reference contains.

almanac: up-to-date information about famous people; facts, figures, charts, and tables about current events, sports, weather, and awards; printed each year

dictionary: listing of words in alphabetical order; gives meanings, spellings, parts of speech, and pronunciations

atlas: maps bound into a book; may also include tables, charts, and information about places in the world, climate, landforms, and population

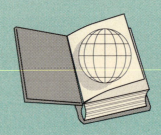

encyclopedia: information on many topics; arranged in volumes; articles, called entries, listed in alphabetical order

Use the information above to answer each question. Fill in the circle in front of the best answer.

1. Which two reference books list their entries in alphabetical order?
   - Ⓐ atlas and dictionary
   - Ⓑ dictionary and encyclopedia
   - Ⓒ almanac and dictionary
   - Ⓓ almanac and encyclopedia

2. Which reference book is published every year?
   - Ⓐ almanac
   - Ⓑ atlas
   - Ⓒ dictionary
   - Ⓓ encyclopedia

3. You want to find out about Spanish explorers in the sixteenth and seventeenth centuries. Where would you look?
   - Ⓐ almanac
   - Ⓑ atlas
   - Ⓒ dictionary
   - Ⓓ encyclopedia

Name _____

After you read

4. In which two reference books would you look to find out the location of the West Indies?
   - Ⓐ almanac and atlas
   - Ⓑ atlas and encyclopedia
   - Ⓒ dictionary and encyclopedia
   - Ⓓ almanac and encyclopedia

5. You want to find out the meaning of the word *indigo*. Where would you look?
   - Ⓐ almanac
   - Ⓑ atlas
   - Ⓒ dictionary
   - Ⓓ encyclopedia

6. You want to learn in what year Hurricane Alice hit Florida. Where would you look?
   - Ⓐ almanac
   - Ⓑ atlas
   - Ⓒ dictionary
   - Ⓓ encyclopedia

7. Where would you look to find out what types of goods the Spaniards brought back on their ships?
   - Ⓐ almanac
   - Ⓑ atlas
   - Ⓒ dictionary
   - Ⓓ encyclopedia

8. You want to find out how far the coast of Florida is from Spain. Where would you look?
   - Ⓐ almanac
   - Ⓑ atlas
   - Ⓒ dictionary
   - Ⓓ encyclopedia

9. Where would you look to find out the price of gold in 1985?
   - Ⓐ almanac
   - Ⓑ atlas
   - Ⓒ dictionary
   - Ⓓ encyclopedia

10. Where would you look to find a table that shows wind currents off the coast of Florida?
    - Ⓐ almanac
    - Ⓑ atlas
    - Ⓒ dictionary
    - Ⓓ encyclopedia

11. You want to find out how ships were built in the 1700's. Where would you look?
    - Ⓐ almanac
    - Ⓑ atlas
    - Ⓒ dictionary
    - Ⓓ encyclopedia

12. You want to know the population of Florida in 1988. Where would you look?
    - Ⓐ almanac
    - Ⓑ atlas
    - Ⓒ dictionary
    - Ⓓ encyclopedia

STRIDES "Treasure Beneath the Sea," pages 190–207
Study Skills: Reference Sources

After you read

Name _____

Often a writer will show a cause-and-effect relationship within one paragraph. The paragraph will tell the reader what happened and why it happened.

Write a paragraph for your classmates that shows several effects for a given cause.

Prewriting

Imagine that you found a buried treasure worth millions of dollars.

▶ What effect would it have on you?
▶ What would you do with the money?
▶ How would it change your life?

In the boxes below, make a list of three results that come to your mind.

Cause: *found treasure worth millions of dollars*

Effect:

Effect:

Effect:

132

STRIDES "Treasure Beneath the Sea," pages 190–207
Language: Paragraph That Shows Cause-and-Effect Relationships

Name _____

 **Composing**

Use your map on page 132 to write a paragraph that tells what would happen if you were to find buried treasure. Remember to give at least three effects that this treasure would have on your life.

_____
_____
_____
_____
_____
_____
_____
_____
_____
_____
_____
_____
_____

Revising Checklist
- ☐ Read your paragraph to yourself or to a partner.
- ☐ Think about your audience and your purpose. Add or cut information.
- ☐ Check to see that your paragraph gives at least three effects.
- ☐ Check for wordy language.

Proofreading Checklist
- ☐ Check for errors in capitalization.
- ☐ Check to see that your paragraph is indented.
- ☐ Circle any words you think are misspelled.
- ☐ Find out how to spell them correctly.

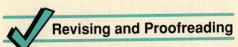 **Revising and Proofreading**

Use the **Revising Checklist** and the **Proofreading Checklist** to help you make changes. Then use your best handwriting to copy your paragraph onto a clean sheet of paper. Check to make sure that you copied your paragraph correctly.

 **Publishing**

Share your paragraph with a classmate. Together, compare and contrast the effects that the treasure would have on each of you.

STRIDES "Treasure Beneath the Sea," pages 190–207
Language: Paragraph That Shows Cause-and-Effect Relationships

After you read

Name _____

Sometimes your purpose for reading will be to collect information. If you know what information you are looking for, you can *scan* the material to find it quickly. Once you find the information, write it down. Then put together, or *organize*, the information so that it will be useful.

Scan the selection "Students Working: Getting the Job Done" to find which jobs are mentioned. Then follow the directions and answer the questions. Write the answers on the lines.

1. Find all the jobs that are mentioned in the selection. List the jobs on the lines below. Then work with some classmates to think of two other jobs. Add them to the list.

    ▶ _____
    ▶ _____
    ▶ _____
    ▶ _____
    ▶ _____
    ▶ _____
    ▶ _____

2. Organize the jobs you have listed into the two categories shown below. Write the jobs that belong in each category.

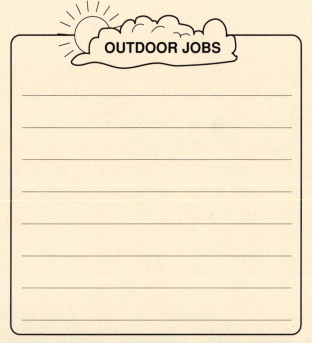

STRIDES   "Students Working: Getting the Job Done," pages 208–213
Comprehension: Organizing and Categorizing Information

Name _____

3. Here are three different categories for organizing the information. Write the jobs that fit in each category.

4. Organize the jobs by deciding whether they require physical labor or mental labor. Some jobs may require both.

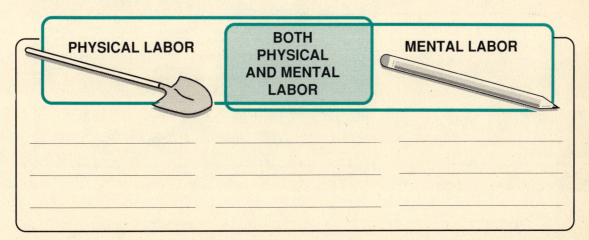

5. Rank the jobs from the one you think you would enjoy doing most to the one you think you would enjoy doing least.

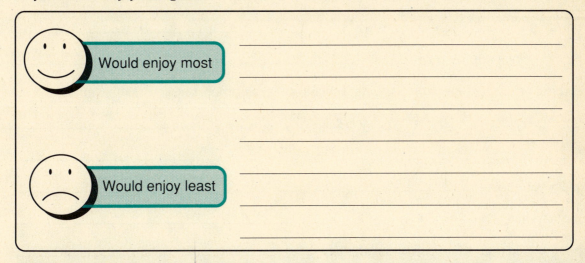

After you read

Name _____

The *classified section* of the newspaper has advertisements for jobs. The cost of advertisements is based on the number of words. Therefore, people include only the most important information and leave out words that are not necessary. Words are often abbreviated.

Here are some common abbreviations used in newspaper advertisements.

w/	with		yr.	year
refs.	references		M-F	Monday through Friday
exp.	experience		asst.	assistant
nec.	necessary		ext.	extension
wk.	week		eves.	evenings
hr.	hour			
mo.	month			

Read the classified advertisements below and answer the questions.

556 HELP WANTED

- Babysitting, afternoon 4-6, M-F, $2.00 per hr., refs. 555-9930, ext. 41, Margie.
- Drummer needed. Eves. $8 per hr. 3 yrs. exp. nec. Call Jason, 555-4433.
- Lead singer for serious top-40 band, leave message: 555-4433.
- Bookkeeper for large music store. M-F, 9-5, 2 yrs. exp. nec. $900 per mo., 555-9988 days.

556 HELP WANTED

- Nurses needed. Immediate openings on 7-3 shift. Must be certified. 2 wks. vacation per yr. Northwood Nursing Center, 555-7010.
- Part-time office help wanted. 8-noon, M-F. No exp. nec. $4.50 per hr. 555-6933, Mr. Taylor.

1. You would like to be a drummer with a band. What number will you dial to find out about the job? _____

2. You want a part-time job after school. Which job has the right hours for you? _____ How much does the job pay? _____
What days and hours would you work? _____

3. Which two jobs are full-time? _____

4. You think you would like to work in an office for the summer, but you take swimming lessons every day at 1:00 P.M. What job might be right for you? _____
_____

Explain your answer. _____

What days and hours would you work? _____

Whom should you call to ask about the job? _____

STRIDES Students Working: "Getting the Job Done," pages 208–213
Study Skills: Newspaper Advertisements

Name _____

WORDS I HAVE LEARNED

WORD	MEANING / SENTENCE

STRIDES
Words I Have Learned

Name _____

WORDS I FREQUENTLY MISSPELL

_____	_____	_____
_____	_____	_____
_____	_____	_____
_____	_____	_____
_____	_____	_____
_____	_____	_____
_____	_____	_____
_____	_____	_____
_____	_____	_____
_____	_____	_____
_____	_____	_____
_____	_____	_____
_____	_____	_____

STUDY STEPS TO LEARN A WORD

Follow these steps when you wish to learn to spell a word correctly.

SAY the word. Recall when you have heard the word used. Think about what it means.

LOOK at the word. Find any prefixes, suffixes, or other word parts you know. Think about other words that are related in meaning and spelling. Try to picture the word in your mind.

SPELL the word to yourself. Think about the way each sound is spelled. Notice any unusual spelling.

WRITE the word while looking at it. Check the way you have formed your letters. If you have not written the word clearly or correctly, write it again.

CHECK your learning. Cover the word and write it. If you did not spell the word correctly, practice these steps until the word becomes your own.

Name _____

Learning Log

THOUGHTS AND IDEAS FROM MY READING

Name _____

THOUGHTS AND IDEAS FROM MY READING